Routledge Revivals

What's in a Name?

First Published in 1970, *What's in a Name* is intended for the layman who feels some curiosity about local names and would like to know more about them- their history, the clues they hold to the life of the past, and the methods of discovering what they have to tell. Place-names can, as the authors of this book put it, 'help to unravel the beginnings of English history'. Books on place-names tend, in the main, to concentrate upon technical linguistic matters, but this book, while not neglecting the technical aspect of the subject, places more emphasis on history at large.

It is designed as a popular introduction to the study of place- names and the authors describe the pleasure to be derived from knowledge of the history and meaning of place-names, showing how they can illuminate battles and settlements, the occupations and beliefs of men and women, the sides of castles and of Roman roads. Those who travel about the countryside will find this to enrich their enjoyment of England.

What's in a Name?

C. Stella Davies and John Levitt

First published in 1970
by Routledge & Kegan Paul Ltd.

This edition first published in 2024 by Routledge
4 Park Square, Milton Park, Abingdon, Oxon, OX14 4RN

and by Routledge
605 Third Avenue, New York, NY 10017

Routledge is an imprint of the Taylor & Francis Group, an informa business

© 1970 C. Stella Davies and John Levitt

All rights reserved. No part of this book may be reprinted or reproduced or utilised in any form or by any electronic, mechanical, or other means, now known or hereafter invented, including photocopying and recording, or in any information storage or retrieval system, without permission in writing from the publishers.

Publisher's Note
The publisher has gone to great lengths to ensure the quality of this reprint but points out that some imperfections in the original copies may be apparent.

Disclaimer
The publisher has made every effort to trace copyright holders and welcomes correspondence from those they have been unable to contact.

A Library of Congress record exists under ISBN: 0710067534

ISBN: 978-1-032-83053-7 (hbk)
ISBN: 978-1-003-50751-2 (ebk)
ISBN: 978-1-032-83054-4 (pbk)

Book DOI 10.4324/9781003507512

What's in a Name?

C. Stella Davies and John Levitt

London
ROUTLEDGE & KEGAN PAUL

*First published in 1970
by Routledge & Kegan Paul Ltd
Broadway House, 68–74 Carter Lane
London, E.C.4*

*Printed in Great Britain
by Clarke, Doble & Brendon Ltd,
Plymouth*

© *C. Stella Davies and John Levitt 1970*

*No part of this book may be reproduced
in any form without permission from
the publisher, except for the quotation
of brief passages in criticism*

ISBN 0 7100 6753 4

Foreword

This book is intended for the layman who feels some curiosity about local names and would like to know more about them—their history, the clues they hold to the life of the past, and the methods of discovering what they have to tell. We felt that there was a need for a popular introduction to this field, in which there was rather less concentration upon technical linguistic matters, and rather more upon history at large, than is perhaps usual in place-name books. We hope we have succeeded in providing one.

Our academic debts will be obvious. No writer on this subject can avoid being immeasurably in the debt of Ekwall. The two splendid volumes of *English Place-Name Elements* by A. H. Smith have been repeatedly invaluable. The books which we recommend to the reader on pp. 102-104 have been also helpful to us.

We have more personal debts too: to Olive Hitchcock, and to Joan Levitt, who read our chapters and were helpful in their comments; and to Vicky Steventon, who typed most of the manuscript.

It remains to say that this has been a genuine collaboration, with the work very evenly divided. In general, Stella Davies is responsible for the historical content of the book, and John Levitt for the philological. In detail, we worked together so closely that if the reader should discover errors we should both find it hard to say which of us should be blamed. Errors we can hardly hope to avoid, but we hope they are both slight and few.

C. Stella Davies
John Levitt

Contents

		page
1	Preliminaries	1
2	The Earliest Known Place-names	10
3	The Coming of the English	25
4	The Spread of Settlement	33
5	Religion and Superstition	43
6	The Coming of the Vikings	54
7	The Normans and After	70
8	Curiosities	82
9	Place-names and the English Language	92
	Taking it Further	102
	Index of Place-names	105

Maps

Old English Place-names in -ingas	27
Place-names incorporating the names of Pagan Gods	46
Place-names ending in -by	58

Chapter 1
Preliminaries

Signposts, giving place-names, stand everywhere about the English country-side directing travellers to cities, towns, and villages. Most counties have name-boards to mark their boundaries; and some of the more helpful also label streams and rivers. In hill and walking country we are helped by pointers marking the 'Footpath to Hellvellyn', or to Kinder Scout, or to Dunkery Beacon. Indeed, public footpaths all over the country are now being sign-posted more systematically, as a result of legislation (1965) passed to preserve traditional rights of way. The main purpose of all this labelling is of course to inform the traveller where he is, or how to get to where he wants to go; but the place-names themselves can have another use. They can help to unravel the beginnings of English history.

Even a slight knowledge of the history and meaning of place-names will relieve the tedium of a long car run or train journey; and be an excellent alternative to the cross-word puzzle. A glance at a sign-post, a map and a place-names dictionary are all that is needed for a beginning. A wider and deeper knowledge of the subject will later bring increasing reward. The past comes alive and the landscape is imbued with the memory of men and women, long dead, whose names and works live on in the names of cities, townships, and hamlets. For instance, Beornwulf, after whom the village of Barlaston in Staffordshire takes its name; Bada, who had a wood at Bathurst in Sussex; Sighulf, a Scandinavian who had a thorn-bush at Sigglesthorne in East Yorkshire; these are a few, remembered at random. Mostly, little more than their names can be known. But some were kings, some bishops. In a less personal way, there are other things to be learnt. The natural features of the country, the hills and streams, woods and coppices, may preserve in their names the speech of a people whose kingdoms were established before the Romans came. *Cannock* in Staffordshire, for instance, is a name which comes down from a

Preliminaries

British hill-name, as does *Conock* in Wiltshire, and the first part of *Consett* in Durham. (The second part of Consett is the English word *head*; it occurs in this form also in the surname Blackett.)

The vast majority of English place-names are over a thousand years old, and a few of them must be nearly two thousand. In that time there have been great changes in the way they were pronounced, as there have been also in the languages from which they were formed. Most of the time the names have existed, the occasions when it was necessary to write them down on paper would not have arisen very often. The written word has become as dominant as it now is only in the last few centuries; the names are much older than that. Nevertheless, the written forms of the names are the best evidence we have for the history of the names themselves.

This of course raises a problem: the spellings that come down to us need interpreting. What pronunciation does an early place-name spelling indicate? Cedelintone, for instance, was the spelling in the *Domesday Book* of a place which is now Chillington, in Staffordshire. Was the first *c* 'hard' (as in cold) or 'soft' (as in cistern)—or perhaps, like *ch* in chimney? How were the letters— *tone* pronounced? These might seem merely academic questions, but in fact they are very important. Language exists in speech, and spelling, particularly in such early times as this, is no more than a reflection of speech. To find out what the name meant, we have to know what it sounded like. 'How do I know what I mean until I hear what I say?'—this question is not so silly as it seems; it has been found from long experience to be the basic question for the philologist—the man who studies the writings of the past.

The interpretation of place-names is a specialist's business. In most cases, the specialist can arrive at a satisfactory solution to the problems a name might raise, and so reveal the original meanings of the word or words which were used to make the name. Some mysteries remain, however. We shall notice one or two of these later in this book.

There is one important fact that becomes clear, as the meanings of place-names are revealed: places were never named fancifully. Today, when marketing a new detergent or occupying a new semi-detached bungalow, one may allow oneself some whimsical experiment. In the early days, however, names were given for purely practical reasons: to identify a site, by describing

Preliminaries

it or naming its owner. Place-names start life as ordinary words. They have in most cases ceased to look like them (but names like Greenfield, Westwood, or Hightown are clear enough in meaning); this is because the words in normal use in the language as a whole have been subjected to different influences than those same words when formed into place-names: words and names have developed apart. But they retain their common origins.

It is often possible therefore to see behind the name the character of the district as it was when the early settlers arrived, the changes which took place as the result of the various invasions, and the uses to which the land was put around the newly founded homes. Place-names supply clues about the survival of preceding peoples; and through them, too, we have glimpses of the culture of the past. They offer evidence for many periods of history, but they are particularly useful for eking out our knowledge of the Anglo-Saxon invasions of the Dark Ages, a period for which we have little documentary evidence.

It might be helpful at this point to outline, briefly, the various peoples who have occupied the land of England, together with their various languages, as a preliminary to the chapters which follow in which each phase of the history of place-names will be discussed in more detail.

The first inhabitants of the country whom it is important to touch on were the Celtic peoples who were in possession before the Romans first came in 54 BC. These peoples were not dispossessed; they remained as subjects of the Romans whilst Britain formed part of the Roman Empire, and were still here when the Anglo-Saxons arrived in the fifth century. It will be convenient to notice them again after mentioning the Romans themselves.

Although the Romans occupied this country for nearly 400 years—from their coming in the first century AD to some time in the first quarter of the fifth century—only a few place-names given by them have survived in use, though many are in fact known. This is largely because the succeeding invaders, the Angles, Jutes and Saxons, seem not to have moved into Roman cities. They chose new sites on which to set up their villages; their way of life was rural rather than urban. (It seems, though, that they sometimes cultivated land which had been ploughed by their predecessors.) The Roman cities themselves, with a few exceptions—London, for instance, and Canterbury—were disused

Preliminaries

and allowed to fall into ruins. They were seldom reoccupied before the lapse of some centuries; and some, indeed, were never reoccupied at all.

Where a Roman place-name survived in living use, it was transmitted through the language of peoples who spoke Celtic; or Old English; or a Scandinavian language. (Latin—the language of the Roman legions—ceased to be spoken in this country when the legions left.) In the course of this, the name was often reinterpreted. The name York is an example; the Old English form of it was Eofor-wic, or 'boar village'. This was an attempt to make sense of a Latin name 'Eboracum', which means something else. (In fact, the Latin form is itself a Romanized version of an earlier Celtic name, Eburacon, which might come either from a personal name, or from a word meaning yew-tree. To complete the story, the modern form York is descended from a Scandinavian version of the Old English name Eoforwic; and the word wic, in this Old English name, which means a dwelling, a farm, or a village, is itself an early borrowing from Latin.) Other Roman names which have survived into modern use are London, Sarum (for Salisbury) and perhaps the first part of the name Portsmouth.

The people who lived in this country before the Romans came in the first century AD, whose descendants lived through the Roman occupation and also survived it, were the British, as we have said. They are popularly referred to as the 'Ancient Britons', though this name gives a misleading impression of their state of civilization. After the departure of the Romans they are normally called the 'Romano-British'. They spoke a Celtic language which in various forms is still spoken in Scotland (Gaelic), in Ireland (Erse) and, more widely, in Wales.

Names left by the Romans may be few, but there are many which survive from the Celts. Many of them are names of natural features of the landscape, such as rivers and hills. It is not possible to say precisely when these Celtic names were given. It could have been at any time between 500 BC and the fifth century AD. They have come down to us through the Anglo-Saxons, who often combined these names with words or syllables from their own language. Celtic names, and hybrids of Celtic and Anglo-Saxon elements, will be discussed in chapter 2.

The Angles, Jutes and Saxons who invaded this country in the fifth century were Germanic tribes who are collectively re-

Preliminaries

ferred to as the Anglo-Saxons. The language they spoke was also, formerly, called 'Anglo-Saxon'. This term can still be found in old text-books and dictionaries; but the language is in fact English, though not English as we know it. It is 'Old English'; and this is the term that will be used in this book.

At one time it was believed that the Romano-British (Celtic) inhabitants of the country were exterminated by the Anglo-Saxons, or thrust farther and farther westward until they survived only in Wales and Cornwall. Modern research, partly based upon place-names, has modified this view. Many place-names referring to natural features remained in use even in those parts of England which were subject to the first and fiercest onslaught of the invaders—the east and the south. The rivers Ouse, Trent, and the Thames were among the waterways along which the Anglo-Saxon war-bands first entered this country, and it is on their banks that some of the first settlements were made. Yet the names of these rivers are Celtic in origin, and must have been passed on to the conquerors by the conquered: who must therefore have survived, to come to be on speaking terms with their enemies.

Pen, in Buckinghamshire, has a Celtic name meaning a hilltop. It is surrounded by towns with Old English names—High Wycombe, Aylesbury, Chesham, Beaconsfield. It may be that a group of the defeated British occupied the wooded slopes of Pen during the Anglo-Saxon settlement of the surrounding countryside. Gildas, who wrote an account of the miserable fate of the British in the fifth century, records that 'they fled to the woods and hills'.

As one would expect, Celtic place-names survive in greater numbers towards the west until in Wales, and to a lesser degree in Cornwall, the majority of names are Celtic.

In the hill country of the north and west of England, the evidence of place-names suggests that the ways of life of Celts and Anglo-Saxons more or less complemented each other. The Anglo-Saxon economy was based upon corn-growing, helped out by the keeping of livestock; Celtic economy, upon the keeping of livestock, helped out by a little corn-growing. The Anglo-Saxons therefore sought first the lands which the Celts did not need. Celtic settlements could survive on the spacious pastures of the hill country, whilst at the same time the Anglo-Saxons were laying out their ploughland on the clay-covered plains below. The

Preliminaries

situation at Pen might therefore have been repeated more frequently in Lancashire, Cheshire, and along the borders of Wales.

There is another reason for the survival of many Celtic place-names, or of Celtic elements within English place-names. When the Anglo-Saxon invaders reached the western parts of England, it was already over one hundred years since their ancestors had first arrived, in the east and the south of the land. The fury of the conflict with the British had abated; and, once over the watershed of the midland plain and the Pennines, the movement of settlement was more a steady colonization than a military invasion. On this point, the *Anglo-Saxon Chronicle* offers some help. The *Chronicle*, which is a compilation of tradition, history, and contemporary record, was put together in the ninth century; but it includes historical accounts of an earlier date. It recounts many conflicts and battles between the British and the Anglo-Saxons in the south and east, but none in the west. Indeed, in one account of a battle between two Anglo-Saxon kingdoms which took place near Leeds in the year 633 (almost two hundred years since the first invasion), British warriors are recorded as allies of the Anglo-Saxon king of Mercia against the Anglo-Saxon king of Northumbria. The name of Leeds is of Celtic origin; the place was part of a British kingdom which endured far beyond the time of this battle. It appears, therefore, that Anglo-Saxons and British could in some circumstances come to terms with each other, and live side by side without war.

This point has been set out in some detail because it is interesting for the traveller to work out the connection between the number of Celtic place-names, the historical sequence of the Anglo-Saxon invasion, and the geographical conditions. In lowland country the place-names will be mainly Anglo-Saxon, with occasional Celtic names, which become more frequent towards the west. In hilly country, especially if it is well-wooded, Celtic names will be less rare, even towards the east.

Over England as a whole, Anglo-Saxon place-names account for about two-thirds of the total number. Most of them date from the period between the fifth and the eleventh centuries. In their various historical forms they have been used for the same places ever since. The sites the Anglo-Saxons chose to live in are still occupied today. The way in which towns, villages and hamlets of England are arranged—the pattern of settlement—still owes a very great deal to these, our remote ancestors. They settled throughout the whole country, though not, of course, with the same strength in all parts. There are fewer Old English placenames in proportion to the whole in Cornwall and Cumberland.

The Anglo-Saxons did not come primarily to found a colony, as the Romans had done, to be part of a great empire. Their settlement was more a movement of peoples who, severing their connections with their homeland, sought a place to plant new roots—literally as well as metaphorically. The nearest recent parallel is the gradual encroachment of the Americans over the western prairies. In both instances there were great empty spaces to be occupied; a scanty population of indigenous people to be fought, conquered and displaced; and lands to be won for a living.

These intentions are reflected in place-names. Some names are names of habitations—names ending in -ham, and -ton, for instance, words which, when not used in place-names, developed into the modern words 'home' and 'town'—though the latter word, in its earliest uses, meant something much smaller than a modern town. Others are names of pastures, of forest clearings, of cow-sheds, and even of pig-sties, as well as of cultivated lands. Beyond the circle of each settlement there would be woods, forests, and moorlands, each also given an Old English name, or perhaps called by a borrowed Celtic name. We have noticed how the names of many natural features are of Celtic origin; but many of them of course are also Old English. Many people must have been puzzled by the word 'low' used in the name of a hill—as in Hounslow, Bromlow, and Mucklow. This goes back to the Old English 'hlaw', a word by which the Anglo-Saxons usually referred to a burial-mound either found by them on their arrival, or made by them later. In different parts of the country the word became low, law, or occasionally ley; the differences are differences of dialect arising later. Again, many river-names are Celtic; but there are also many Old English.

The countryside, in short, reflects the intentions and achievements of the Anglo-Saxons; and no less so when its features were those they inherited from the Celts and Romans. The Roman roads were part of that heritage; and many, like Watling Street, received Old English names. So too did many of the Roman forts and towns—edifices which, not yet fallen as completely into ruin as they since became, were things at which the Anglo-Saxons

Preliminaries

could marvel. 'The work of giants,' as an Anglo-Saxon poet said when standing before the walls of, possibly, Bath.

The fourth group of invaders to occupy England were the Scandinavians. From the middle of the eighth until the eleventh century, England was afflicted by raids and invasion from these peoples—who spoke various dialects of the Old Norse language which later became the modern languages of Norway, Sweden, Denmark and Iceland. The early raids were smash-and-grab affairs launched for the sake of plunder; but as time went on the invaders increasingly remained here and set up homes. The pattern of settlement was very uneven. In the eastern counties from the Scottish border to the Thames, Scandinavian names are to be found in quantity; in the Lake District they are in the majority; and there are many on the sea-board of Lancashire and Cheshire. In other districts there are none at all.

This pattern was the result of attack and defence, treaty and compromise. The Anglo-Saxons found it impossible to expel the Scandinavians; but, historically speaking, they were rather quickly assimilated. Their way of life was not greatly different from that of the Anglo-Saxons, and they quite readily accepted the Christian religion. This is not to say that there was not much fighting, ravage and bloodshed; but the result was in the nature of a stalemate. Neither side was conquered; each learned to tolerate the other.

This situation is reflected in place-names. Some give evidence of the measures taken by the Anglo-Saxons to contain the Scandinavians. The place-name ending -bury or -borough is descended from an Old English word 'burh'. This usually referred to a stronghold, or fortified place, and a number of places whose names contain it are known to have been fortified by the English against the Scandinavians. An example is Eddisbury, in Cheshire. Other evidence illustrates not conflict, but co-existence: typical Scandinavian names and typical Anglo-Saxon names occur side by side in many eastern counties. (A Scandinavian place-name ending is -by; it is instructive to see how names ending in this may be scattered amongst typical Old English place-names in -ham or -ton, in many eastern counties.) Some names give more striking evidence of assimilation of Scandinavian, Anglo-Saxon and occasionally British communities; these contain elements from the several languages compounded together. Stainley, for instance, is a compound of Old English and Scandi-

Preliminaries

navian; so is Holbeck. Penkridge is Old English and British; so is Lichfield.

Celtic, Roman, Old English and Scandinavian: this is the historical sequence of place-name settlement. These people and their languages account for the overwhelming number of place-names in present-day use. The Norman Conquest resulted in a handful being added, and the gradual increase in places of habitation, and changes in the use of land, in the subsequent centuries, added a few more, but there were not many. A few places have names as late as the nineteenth and twentieth centuries; but these are also rare.

There is one final point to add, to complete this introduction. Place-names form a substantial number of our surnames. Generally speaking, until the end of the fourteenth century, for most people, one name was enough. This was a truly personal name—the 'given' name, or, the name known after Baptism as the christian name. (It is still the only name the English Church is concerned with.) But as time went on, and communities grew larger, and the need to keep records grew more demanding, one name was no longer enough. Already, before 1066, people were being identified by an addition to their personal name: adding to it, for instance, the name of their father (Harold Godwinsson); later on we find the use of a nickname (for instance, James Short); or some indication of their employment (John Clark; James Millar, etc.). Very often this additional name was some indication of the place where they lived, or from which they came—Allen Dale, for instance; or Robert Churchill. These last two sorts are most relevant to our subject; they are, first, topographical names (Hill, Wood, Bridges, etc.) and second, names of definable places (Leeds, Bradford, Longbottom). Fathers' names, nicknames, occupation names, or place-names—from being occasional additions to a person's given name, they came to be permanent second names inherited in the modern way. The story of names is not only the story of place-names, but also of personal names.

Chapter 2
The Earliest Known Place-names

For many centuries before the Christian era this country was periodically invaded by many and different people. They have left tools and weapons buried in the river drift of ancient valleys, in caves, and at their squatting places. Neolithic men—men of the new stone age—and the later metal-using people built long or round barrows in which to bury their dead, and some of these have remained. A few of their villages have been identified. Those in Anglesey and at Skara Brae in Orkney have quite recognizable huts and streets. These villages and the natural features of the districts around them must have been given names by these early peoples, but their languages are now lost and none of the names have survived in any form that can be recognized. The history of place-names in Britain begins much later, with the Celts.

Who were the Celts? We have already met them in Chapter 1. We must now say more about them. They were tribes who occur in history with various names: the Gauls against whom Caesar made war, the Belgae who invaded part of Britain within the lifetime of people to whom Julius Caesar spoke, the British, and others. They spoke languages closely related to each other; languages which originated as dialects of a common Celtic speech, which itself is one of the main branches of the extensive Indo-European family of languages from which most of the languages of Europe and India have descended. Common Celtic split into two main branches. From the 'Q-Celtic' branch there descended a language known as Goidelic, which was the ancestor of modern Irish, Scottish, and Manx Gaelic. From the 'P-Celtic' branch there developed a language known as Gallo-Brittonic; and, as one might expect from the name, this form of speech was used in Gaul and in mainland Britain. It was at one time believed that the speakers of P-Celtic had arrived somewhat later than the speakers of Q-Celtic, and had dispossessed them from the mainland; but this no longer held. Whatever the details of their move-

The Earliest Known Place-names

ments from Europe into Britain, by the time of the first clear historical records about this land the Celts—the Brittonic Celts—were in occupation.

There is a last movement of Celts to be taken into consideration. The Belgae, who were again Brittonic as opposed to Goidelic speakers, had long been settled in Gaul, and from there, about the year 75 BC, they extended their domain across the Channel and established themselves in various areas in the south-west of Britain. On the continent, they had proved troublesome to the Roman Empire and it was indeed in an attempt to prevent the Belgae of Britain from giving help and refuge to their kindred in Gaul that Caesar made his abortive attempt at invading Britain in 55 BC.

The Celtic-speaking peoples, in particular the Belgae, were skilful users of iron and other metals, and had developed a high culture in tools, weapons, dress and ornament. The Belgae introduced coinage into Britain. Few details are known about the way of life of the Celts as a whole. The Roman writers have left a very biased account, regarding them as untutored savages with curious customs, and in a strange way this impression has survived in the present-day comic-strip conception of the Ancient Briton. It is known that their villages were often stockaded, and their huts were round. They ploughed the land to raise crops of grain, in small square fields which have left marks which can sometimes still be seen on hillsides. For war and conquest they used horse chariots which had knives attached to the wheels. One of these chariots was recently excavated in Anglesey, and is now in Cardiff museum. Numbers of excavated artifacts from the period testify to a high degree of art and skill in handling metals and making pottery. For decoration they used, among other designs, a particularly graceful and flowing line called the 'Celtic curve'. There is the well-known fact, reported by Julius Caesar, that they painted themselves with blue dye, woad. Many fortresses on hill-tops, defended by multiple systems of walls and ditches, testify to the battles fought between the Celtic-speaking tribes for possession of the land, and later to battles between the Celts and the Romans.

We suggested in Chapter 1 that the many Celtic names which have survived into present-day use indicate two things: first, that Celtic was used in this country throughout the Roman occupation; and second, that when the Anglo-Saxon invasions

The Earliest Known Place-names

took place in the fifth century they were not accompanied by a wholesale extermination of Celts as was formerly thought.

In the first century of the Christian era the Romans returned to Britain, and carried through a more effective invasion than they had attempted under Julius Caesar. Britain became a colony of Rome, and remained so for four centuries. The language of Rome was Latin, but how extensively it was spoken in this country is a matter for conjecture. The degree would have varied in different parts of the country; more consistently in the south and east, where Roman civilization was more firmly established, than in the north and west, where evidence of the civilization is thinner on the ground, one must assume. The British must in all areas have continued to use their own tongue, however. And this was not in any case the sort of invasion where one population was supplanted by an entire alien population of colonists. Of course, there would be the arrival of the army, and its administrators and camp followers, and some civil administrators too; but the general aim of the assault was not to plant Romans in Britain, but to make the Britons into Romans. When in the end the Romans withdrew, the Celtic speech survived and the Latin did not; though there would certainly be a number of Latin words incorporated into the Celtic.

In facing the next challenge, Celtic was less successful. After the coming of the English, it has been seen that a considerable number of Celtic names were left, incorporated into the English language; but the speech itself died out in England. It survived, and survives yet, in Wales—though 'survival' is rather too limp a term to use for the flourishing condition of modern Welsh; and it also survived in Cornwall until the early years of the twentieth century. (The story that Dolly Pentreath, who died at Mousehole in 1777, aged a hundred and two, was the last speaker of Cornish, is now abandoned.)

We have suggested that the evidence of place-names shows that Anglo-Saxon colonization was heaviest in the eastern and southern parts of the country; that in general the Celtic settlements, if they were left, were sited on the hill-tops rather than in valleys; and that in the north-west there was apparently a pattern of settlement in which the Celts occupied the higher land and the Anglo-Saxons the valleys. We must now look in more detail at these Celtic names.

The Earliest Known Place-names

River-names

The most numerous Celtic names are to be found in the names of rivers; overall, about two-thirds of our river-names are Celtic. A higher proportion of them are to be found in the north and west than in the south and east. Why did so many river-names survive? In some cases—the cases of larger rivers particularly—it may be that they were sufficiently important as avenues of trade for their names to be part of an international stock of knowledge. Traders from the continent had been visiting Britain for many centuries before the birth of Christ. They would come by sea; and since the greater rivers of a country are the natural gateways for seafarers, they could have become known by name to peoples of many sorts. The Anglo-Saxons were raiders, not traders; but their interest in the inlets into Britain would be none the less for that.

For the smaller rivers and tributaries this argument does not hold. It may be that in the end there is no special explanation to be offered at all. It is however interesting to notice that in North America, where the American Indian languages have suffered a similar fate to Celtic, many rivers both large and small preserve Indian names: the Mississippi; the Missouri; and many others. The stability of river-names is one of the odder facts of history.

The following are some examples of Celtic river-names and their meanings:

AIRE   Probably, 'strong river'
AVON   A word which simply means 'river'. There is a modern Welsh word 'afon' meaning 'water, stream'
DEE   This river seems to have been regarded as a holy river; the Celtic original of the name (Deua) means 'the goddess'. (The city of Chester had the same name in Latin: 'Deva', from the river on which it stands)
OUSE   Like Avon, a British river-name going back to an earlier form whose basic meaning is 'water'. (Not always, however; the Sussex Ouse is not Celtic in origin, but English; and the word meant, not water, but mud)
TRENT   From a British river-name meaning something like 'trespasser'; perhaps an allusion to the river's tendency to flood

The Earliest Known Place-names

CAM   From an adjective *cambo₂ which meant 'crooked'. (Note: the asterisk is a sign that the word-form it marks is a hypothetical form; assumed on good evidence to have existed but not actually found in writing)
CRAY   From a British word meaning 'fresh'
FROME   Fair, fine, brisk
LAVER   There is a modern Welsh word llafar, meaning 'vocal'; the river-name perhaps means something like 'babbling brook'
PEOVER   Bright, beautiful

The above examples are of names which refer to the river itself —either under some general designation such as 'water', or by alluding to its shape or habits (Cam; Trent). Occasionally the reference is less direct. The following river-names refer to the kind of vegetation found along their banks:

DERWENT   A word which was derived from *derva, meaning 'oak'
Other river-names of the same origin are: DARENT, DART, DARWEN
WARREN   This word occurs in the name WARREN BURN, the name of a river in Northumberland. The word BURN is an English addition; the word WARREN comes from a British word for alders. 'The alder stream'
LYMM   From a word for elm tree. 'The river by the elms'

Occasionally the name describes the bed of the river. CERNE, CHAR and CHARN all come from a word meaning 'rock'; familiar to walkers in hill country in the word cairn. CRAKE comes from another Celtic word of the same meaning. The river HAMPS, which forms part of the boundary between Derbyshire and Staffordshire, flows through limestone, and disappears into 'swallows' for part of its course in dry weather. The name 'Hamps' meant 'summer-dry'.

Smaller streams than those we have so far noticed have names of Celtic origin; their numbers vary county by county. In Dorset there are no less than eleven; in Somerset there are eight; in Gloucester four; in Cumberland six. (Again, the counties to the west of England have the highest proportion of these.) Here are three examples of the names of small streams:

ARROW (Herefordshire)   'White, bright'
LEADON (Gloucester, and other counties)   'Broad'
KENN (Devonshire)   Derived from a word meaning 'brilliant'

Hill-names

Leaving rivers, the next most numerous class of Celtic place-names to survive are the names of hills. In many cases the Celtic name has been combined with an English prefix or suffix. The following are words which mean simply 'hill', in the way that Avon and Ouse meant simply 'water' or 'river':

BARR (earlier *barro)   As in Great Barr; Barrock; Bray
CRUC, or CRUG   As in Creech, Crich, Crook, or Crutch
PEN   As in Penn, Pendomer, Pentrich, Penkridge, Penrith

This last example may have brought to mind the name of the Pennines—the largest range of mountains and hills in England. This would however be a mistake. There is no evidence in written form that the name was used at all before the eighteenth century. It is, no doubt, just barely possible that the term though unrecorded was in use much earlier. It may have been bestowed on these hills by the Celts, and taken over by the Anglo-Saxons, and survived underground until it accidentally got into the records only two hundred years ago. Alternatively, it could have been invented by some eighteenth-century linguist with a Celtic bias, deliberately giving a name to a previously anonymous range. A last possibility is that it may have been named after the Apennines, by some gentleman of classical education, or some traveller returned from Italy. Nobody knows.

The bare word 'hill' is found alone no more frequently in its Celtic translation than in the English version; usually it is compounded with some other word, making a more particular meaning. Take MELLOR in Derbyshire. This is plausibly supposed to be akin to the Welsh word Moelfre. The last part of this—fre—is a variant of *bre* which figures in Breedon, and Brewood. The first part of it—Moel—is still a present-day Welsh word, and means 'bare'. Moelfre is the 'bare hill'; and so is Mellor. Malvern means precisely the same, but instead of *fre* we have *bryn*—moelbryn. Bryn also means 'hill'.

To move from bare hills to wooded hills: the Brittonic word for wood is *cet*, which appears in modern Welsh as *coed*, and is familiar to holidaymakers in such names as Bettws-y-coed. Add this to a word meaning 'hill', and the result is Penketh in Lancashire, Pencoyd in Herefordshire, and Penge in Surrey.

The Earliest Known Place-names

It will become increasingly obvious during the reading of this book that a very large number of place-names contain the personal names of particular people; and Celtic hill-names are no exception. An example is the name Kinder—the name of the highest part of the Peak District. This probably includes the British name Cunetio; together again with the word *bre*, in its variant form *fre* : 'Cunetio's Hill.'

We have said that Celtic outposts probably survived on hills, and this may account in some part for the large number of hill names that are Celtic. Again, as with river-names and Celtic names in general, these are more numerous towards the west; and most numerous of all in the border counties, and in Devon and Cornwall. Devon and Cornwall were not conquered by the Anglo-Saxons until fairly late in the invasion period. Devon was probably occupied and added to the kingdom of Wessex about 720; Cornwall remained unoccupied for another century, and was possibly half-independent even a century after that. As we have noted above, the Cornish language—a branch of Celtic—remained in use until the nineteenth century. In these counties Celtic place-names for natural features are very numerous; in Cornwall, they form the overwhelming majority. Devonshire examples are: Bray (bre; hill); Crook (crug); Morchard (great wood); Creedy (a river-name).

In the Lake District of Westmorland and Cumberland, Celtic-speaking communities also remained until, and perhaps after, the Norman Conquest of 1066. The fell name of *Blen* is characteristic of the Lake District. It comes from the Celtic word blaen, and means 'top'. When joined to the word *carn*, which has already occurred in connection with the rocky bottom of rivers such as Cerne, Char, and Charn, and which in this connection may mean a heap of stones generally marking a burial place, we get Blencarn, and Blencathra. The word *cumbo- meant a valley. It was borrowed as a general term by the English, quite apart from its use in Celtic place-names; its modern form is 'coomb'. In the north, it is the Celtic form which is most usual; and it is found in Cumrew (the valley by the hill); Cumwhitton (Quintin's valley) and Cundall. This last has had an explanatory last syllable, -dalr, added to it much later in the Norse language spoken by the Scandinavians who invaded the Lake District in the ninth and tenth centuries. Dalr also means *valley* and is related to the modern English word *dale*. (We shall see later that the Scandi-

The Earliest Known Place-names

navians were responsible for many Lake District place-names, almost swamping the original Celtic. Nevertheless, and surprisingly, one feature of Celtic speech survived there—the Celtic numbers (one, two, three, etc.). Within living memory sheep were counted in these numbers on the fell farms of Westmorland and Cumberland: yan, tan, tethera, etc.)

District and County Names

A number of district and county names in England are of Celtic origin.

DEVON   A tribal name, applied to the territory in which the tribe lived. The tribe was the Dumnonii

CORNWALL   This is a blend; the ending -wall is English, going back to *wealas*, which meant 'Welsh'. (Precisely what 'Welsh' meant is another story.) Corn- is Celtic; it goes back to *Cornavia, from another tribal name, Cornovii—the people of the promontory; a very appropriate name for the inhabitants of a peninsula with a rocky coast

KENT   This has been the point of entry of many invasions. It still retains its Celtic name, for which there are three possible meanings. It may be 'the border country', from Celtic *canto*; or 'open country', from Celtic *caint*; or, in another meaning of *canto*, 'white'. All meanings would suit the topography. The white cliffs of Dover, perhaps, make the last interpretation the more probable

THANET   Bright island; fire island. Perhaps from a beacon or a lighthouse

WIGHT   This is certainly Celtic, since it occurs in the writing of Pliny, dating from the Roman period. The meaning is not certain but Ekwall thinks it may be something like 'what has been raised'; that is, an island

CRAVEN (Yorkshire)   This is possibly, but not certainly, Celtic; and it may be derived from a word meaning 'garlic'

ELMET (Yorkshire)   This was the name for an ancient British tribal territory which remained as an isolated kingdom until the seventh century. The origin is obscure. A form Elfet occurs in Welsh records; and there is a personal name derived from it discovered in an inscription in Caernarvon: Elmetiacos

LINDSEY (Lincolnshire)   This is a composite place-name, of which the second part is English—a word meaning 'island'. The first part is British, and comes from a form of *Lindon*, the name

The Earliest Known Place-names

of the place now called Lincoln. Before the fens were drained Lindsey was almost an island

Towns and Larger Villages

The tribal organization of the Ancient British people, and their type of agriculture, did not incline them to urban life. Most of the British lived in the country-side, and large places of habitation were exceptional. Nevertheless, from the researches of archaeologists and from the few records of Roman writers, helped out by place-name evidence, a few largish villages or even towns can be identified. Some of their names, considerably modified, have survived into modern use. The following are examples:

LONDON   There is evidence in documents for the existence of a British settlement on the Thames at the time of the Roman invasion. In the earliest record the name is Londinium; it is probably related to a word meaning 'wild'. It could have been a personal name first; or perhaps the name of a tribe

LYMPNE (Kent)   The place of the elms; to be compared with the river-name Lymn, noticed earlier. This is the name of a place, but not necessarily of a settlement. Such names are called *nature-names* as distinct from *habitation-names*, though of course habitations often grow up in places which already have nature-names

RECULVER (Kent)   The great headland. This is another nature-name adapted as a habitation-name

CATTERICK (North Riding)   This place is known to have been the headquarters of the northern British tribe of the Brigantes, who gave the Romans a great deal of trouble during the invasion. The chieftain resisted them with determination but his wife, Catamandura, was pro-Roman, and betrayed her husband into their hands. She later went to Rome as a pensioner of the Emperor.

The place-name itself has been variously interpreted. It seems most probably to have come from the Latin word cataract, which means a waterfall; and this could have been a reference to the river now known as the Swale. Borrowed from the Romans by the British, it could have had its first part altered from *cata* to *catu* (a Celtic word meaning 'war'). Early spellings suggest this.

CARLISLE is a name with a complicated history. It was first a British fortress, one of many built along the narrow stretch of country between the Solway and the Tyne. The Romans knew it

The Earliest Known Place-names

as Luguvallium; a name perhaps derived from a personal name. The Celtic prefix caer-, meaning a fort, was added; and by various alterations and shortenings the modern form emerged over a period of some centuries.

Occasionally we can infer the existence of British settlements from historical records, even though their names are lost. Everybody knows the story of Boudicca, or Boadicea, which was recorded by Tacitus. A statue to her, by a fairly recent sculptor who certainly never knew what she looked like, stands by Westminster Bridge. She resisted the Roman annexation of her territory which lay in what is now East Anglia. Her headquarters were at Camulodunum, which is now Colchester. She was defeated and was treated with great indignity by the Roman officials, being stripped and beaten with rods. Boudicca called her tribesmen, the Iceni, to arms; all the British tribes of eastern England joined them; and there was a great massacre of Romans, in which the Ninth Legion was cut to pieces, and the three towns of Londinium (London), Verulamium (St Albans) and Camulodunum were sacked and destroyed. It was said that as many as seventy thousand people were slain in the rebellion. (The Roman vengeance afterwards was no less terrible.)

This tragic episode, a tiny fragment of the struggle between British and invading Roman which the chance of record has preserved, enables us to see the Celtic origin of Colchester and St Albans—facts which we could hardly have deduced from the present names. A considerable population in East Anglia can also be inferred. There must have been many fairly large centres of habitation whose names have been lost to us. It would be wrong, in other words, to estimate the size of the British population by the number of their place-names which have survived.

Finally, two composite types of name which have Celtic elements. Manchester will serve as an example of the first type, and is typical of many names which end in -chester or -caster. The word 'chester' is an English word, added by the Anglo-Saxons to many previously existing names, often Celtic, to indicate the existence of a Roman fortress or city. (The fact that, in origin, 'chester' entered English from Latin is a complication that makes little difference to the present case. It was borrowed by the Anglo-Saxons in their continental period, and was an established part of their language before they ever came to Britain.) In the case of Manchester the Romano-British name was

The Earliest Known Place-names

Mamucion. The first syllable perhaps comes from a Celtic word 'mame', a breast; and may refer to the rounded hills which surround the centre of Manchester on one of which the British settlement probably stood.

The second type is that in which the English suffix -bury is added to a Celtic name. Bury is a form of the Old English burh, which means a fortified place. When it is found joined with a Celtic name it suggests that the fortress itself was British. Countisbury, in Devon, is a name of this type. The first part comes from the British 'Cunet', which is related to an adjective meaning 'high'. Another example is Salisbury. This owes the first part of its name to the Celtic 'Sorvio'; the meaning is not known.

British hill forts are to be found all over England. They were built either to repel invading peoples, or for protection in intertribal warfare. They are numerous along the English Channel, particularly in the west. The most spectacular of them is Maiden Castle, with its very intricate system of defences. But this name itself should underline a warning: though some Celtic forts have names of the Countisbury type, in the majority of cases the name gives no indication of the people who built them, for as with Maiden Castle, succeeding people have renamed them. There is a limit to what linguistic evidence can show; and beyond the limit we must depend on the archaeologist.

Smaller Celtic Settlements

The names of British villages and hamlets have not survived in any great quantity over the larger part of England. They are most numerous in districts where the Celtic language lived on longest after the Anglo-Saxon invasions: Herefordshire, and Cumberland; and, to a lesser extent, Dorset, Wiltshire, Shropshire and Lancashire. The following are examples:

Herefordshire
DINEDOR   The earliest record is in Domesday Book, when the form of the name is Dunre. This is probably 'the village by the hill'
MOCCAS   A moor for pigs
TRETIRE   Rythir in the thirteenth century. Probably 'the long ford'

The Earliest Known Place-names

TREVILLE   Perhaps meaning 'Hamlet with a mill'. Tre in Welsh means 'hamlet'; the second syllable is from 'melin', a mill

Cumberland
CUMDIVOCK   The first syllable means 'valley'; we met it earlier in the section on hill-names. The second element may be a personal name
CUMREW   The valley by the hill. A nature-name not originally the name of a settlement. A village growing up in a valley may take on the name of the valley itself, and though the village may be Anglo-Saxon the valley may have a Celtic name, learnt by the Anglo-Saxons long before the establishment of the village
PENRITH   The chief ford
PENRUDDOCK   The element 'pen' occurs here again; meaning 'chief'. The ending of the name is something of a mystery

Shropshire
ERCALL   The meaning of this name is not known. There are two place-names containing it: High Ercall and Child's Ercall. They are not very near to each other so it is probable that the name applied to a wide area
HODNET   The first element is a word meaning 'pleasant'; the second is identical with the Welsh word *nant*, a valley
PREES   Contains the Welsh word for brushwood; a place where brushwood is found
WENLOCK   The present name, though Celtic, is comparatively late in origin. It means 'the white monastery'. A nunnery was founded at Wenlock in 680 by St Milburg, an Anglo-Saxon princess. There may have been an earlier British community

Cheshire
CREWE   Stepping stones over a ford. Crewood, near Frodsham, has the same name, with the added Old English 'wood'
INCE   An island or water-meadow. At this point the river Mersey is subject to flooding. In the twelfth century a Cistercian monastery near here was compelled to move quarters because of the encroachments of the river
LANDICAN   The church of St Tecan. Tecan is a Celtic personal name; in this case, that of a British saint. (The Welsh word Llan, 'church', is familiar in names such as Llanberis)

The Earliest Known Place-names

WERNETH   A township in north-east Cheshire. A place overgrown with alder trees

LISCARD   The second element is 'carreg', a cliff. The first means 'a hall'. The hall on the cliff

Lancashire

CULCHETH   A retreat in a wood

HAYDOCK   Interesting in that it gives one of the rare clues to British agriculture. It means a corn farm, or a place where barley was grown

PREESE   A brushwood covert; like Prees in Shropshire

PENKETH   The end of the hill

Lancashire is particularly rich in Celtic habitation-names. The syllable 'pen', going back to a British *penno-, and meaning a top, a height, a hill, is often combined with English elements, as in Pendleton and Pendlebury.

The above examples have been taken from counties where Celtic names are more frequent than elsewhere. Isolated examples from other counties are:

WATCHET (Somerset)   This means 'the lower wood'

CAMS (Hampshire)   On Portsmouth harbour; Ekwall assumes that this is the British name of the bay

PENKRIDGE (Staffordshire)   Hill top

With some experience, the traveller can often provisionally identify Celtic names from the look of the word; though confirmation from a place-name dictionary is always advisable. The elements cum, cumb, che, pen, bre, and hen, give pointers.

Most of the names discussed so far have meanings which refer to the features of the countryside, though one or two testify to religious practices and one other gives an indication of British agriculture at the time the place was named. Later place-names very frequently suggest the callings or industries which were carried on in the sites they name, but Celtic names which do this are extremely rare. It is possible that Gawsworth in Cheshire is one of the exceptions. Ekwall writes cautiously about it, but supposes that 'If the Domesday form is trustworthy, the first element appears to be the Welsh "gof", a smith.' Smiths were specialists from the nature of their craft, needing from the start their own workshops, and perhaps always tending to be set apart from the practice of agriculture which went on around them.

The addition of the Old English element 'worth' to the Celtic word for smith seems a very intimate blending; does it indicate the presence of a British smith in this still tiny village when the Anglo-Saxon people arrived there at the end of the sixth century?

The Romans

For nearly four hundred years the Romans occupied this country. They came in the first century as a conquering army. They built fortresses, roads, bridges and a great wall between the Solway and the Tyne. Later, Roman civilians settled here, and established towns and villas or country estates particularly in the southern parts of Britain. Many Roman place-names are recorded in contemporary documents and many more must have been used that were not recorded. Yet very few of them remain in common use today.

An explanation of this depends on the extent to which the Romanized British adopted Latin as their everyday speech; and where they did, how long it survived in the troubled times of the Anglo-Saxon invasions. The extent to which they did adopt Latin must have varied from place to place; but certainly it never replaced Celtic as the normal speech of the bulk of the population. But as we have seen also, place-names are, linguistically, special cases. Even place-names which are apparently Latin are often really Latinized forms of original Celtic names. We have seen that Deva was the Roman name for Chester; but it was itself a name the Romans adopted from Celtic. Most place-names used by the Romans must have been Celtic, and it is not likely that they would ever have attempted any systematic re-naming of the settlements in their British province.

However, the Latin language has given Britain itself two of its names—the name Britain, and the name 'Albion'. The source for the first is the Celtic-Latin Britannia. (The second 'i' in the English version of this is due to a misplacing of the second 'i' in the Latin 'Britannia'.) This means 'the land of the Britons', and 'Briton' itself is connected with the Celtic word for Pict; and, in the very distant origin, may have had some connection with tattooing or painting the body.

Authorities differ about the meaning of 'Albion'. It may come from the Latin 'Albus', an adjective meaning white, and refer to the cliffs of Dover and the chalk downs of the south coast; or, as

The Earliest Known Place-names

Professor Jackson thinks, it may come from a Celtic word meaning 'the world'. If so, it may be 'a very early example of British insularity'.

There are a number of Latin words which were adopted by the Anglo-Saxons as loanwords, and which later came to have an application in place-names. The word 'chester', already noticed, is a good example; it derives from the Latin 'castra', meaning a fort. This example is very old; the English picked it up on the Continent, and brought it to Britain with them. Names containing this element are numerous: Chester, Manchester, Cirencester, Tadcaster, Grantchester, and many others. The variations between the 'ch' and the 'k' sound are significant and will be explained in a later chapter.

The word 'street', found in the name Chester-le-street, and also in Stratford, and Streatham, and other names, is another Latin word adopted as a common noun. The origin here is 'strata', a pavement; and it was applied to the paved Roman roads which the Anglo-Saxons found here.

The study of place-names is not a fruitful source for the history of the Romans in Britain. Roman place-names were submerged, where they occurred, in the incoming flood of English. One important reason, to add to the others suggested above, was that the Anglo-Saxons had a culture very different from the Romans. They came seeking land to cultivate, not cities to live in. They needed names for new villages they were founding. The Roman fortresses and cities were of little use to them. The fortresses were either sacked by barbarians from the north in the interim between the Roman withdrawal and the arrival of the Anglo-Saxons, or they were disregarded as being unsuitable for the Anglo-Saxon style of warfare. Like the towns, they fell into decay, their very names forgotten. Deva, for instance, the great Roman base on the River Dee, which had housed the Twentieth Legion for over three hundred years, is recorded in the *Anglo-Saxon Chronicle* as 'the waste Chester'.

Chapter 3
The Coming of the English

Enough has been said in earlier chapters about the coming of the Anglo-Saxons to make it plain that this was one of the decisive events in the history of this country. Inevitably, it has left its marks upon the place-names of the country-side: it has led to the creation of by far the greater part of the names we now use. The society set up after the invasions, varying as it did from place to place, growing through the following centuries, not without local setbacks, suffering and surviving wars, conversion, invasion by Danes and conquest by Normans; this society was never to be disrupted by events as harshly as that of the British had been by the Romans, nor the Romano-British by the English themselves. We have reached, therefore, a point at which the place-name evidence, without ever ceasing to tantalize by its gaps, is much more plentiful. Accordingly, we shall need several chapters to do what justice we can to the evidence. Later we shall take up some special aspects of the matter. In this chapter we look more closely at the Anglo-Saxons and their arrival.

Anglo-Saxons and Romans

The Anglo-Saxons spoke a Germanic language related fairly closely to that of the Danes, less closely to that of the Romans and the Celts, and most closely of all to that of the Frisians, who dwelt (and dwell) in the islands of north Holland. We said also that this language—for all practical purposes, one single form of speech, with no apparent differences between any Anglian and Saxon versions—had already borrowed words from Latin. This happened in the 'continental' period of English, before the language came to this country. Our example was the word *chester*, used by the Anglo-Saxons for a Roman camp or fortress. We could have added many others, less important for place-name study but interesting for the history of English. (Street, mile,

The Coming of the English

chalk, belt, sack, purple, are other Latin loanwords of this period.) If one thinks of the way in which these borrowings came about, it suggests the possible relationships between the speakers of English and of Latin.

To begin with, the speakers of English—the Anglo-Saxons—were in Roman opinion barbarians; and most obviously they would meet them as enemies. The attacks on the province of Britain made by the Anglo-Saxons were not isolated forays, particular to this island. They were all of a piece with the assaults being made on other frontiers of the Empire by other groups of barbarians—the Huns, the Langobards, the Vandals, the Goths, and other peoples, whose combined efforts were to put an end to the Western Empire altogether, and to lead to the birth of a new Europe out of its remains. Why, in the earlier centuries of the Christian era, the Germanic peoples north of the Imperial frontier should have been so turbulent and dangerous, so continuously on the move, so much in a social and linguistic melting-pot, it is hard to say. Britain was the most exposed province of the Empire, and was even before the departure of the legions in the early fifth century, under severe if sporadic attack, from Saxon pirates along the south-east coast (known as 'the Saxon Shore'). When the legions were withdrawn, the surviving Romanized British leaders were left to face the fury alone.

We should underestimate the complexity of this phase of history, however, if we saw it entirely in terms of Romans versus pirates. The Romans employed large numbers of barbarians in their legions and they also engaged barbarian armies as 'federated' troops, or paid allies, to defend the line against other barbarians. It is conceivable that among the garrisons of the Roman wall and the Saxon shore there were men whose grandsons would come again with the Anglo-Saxon conquerors.

Anglo-Saxons and British

The Rhine frontier was abandoned in the year 406; and Britain seems to have been evacuated by the legions in the same decade. This period of history is the darkest of all, and what comes out of it has an air of legend rather than fact. It is known that in 446 an appeal was made to Rome for help, by the leaders of the Romanized British, among whom may have been Vortigern, a ruler of Kent; this letter, known dramatically as 'the groans of

The Coming of the English

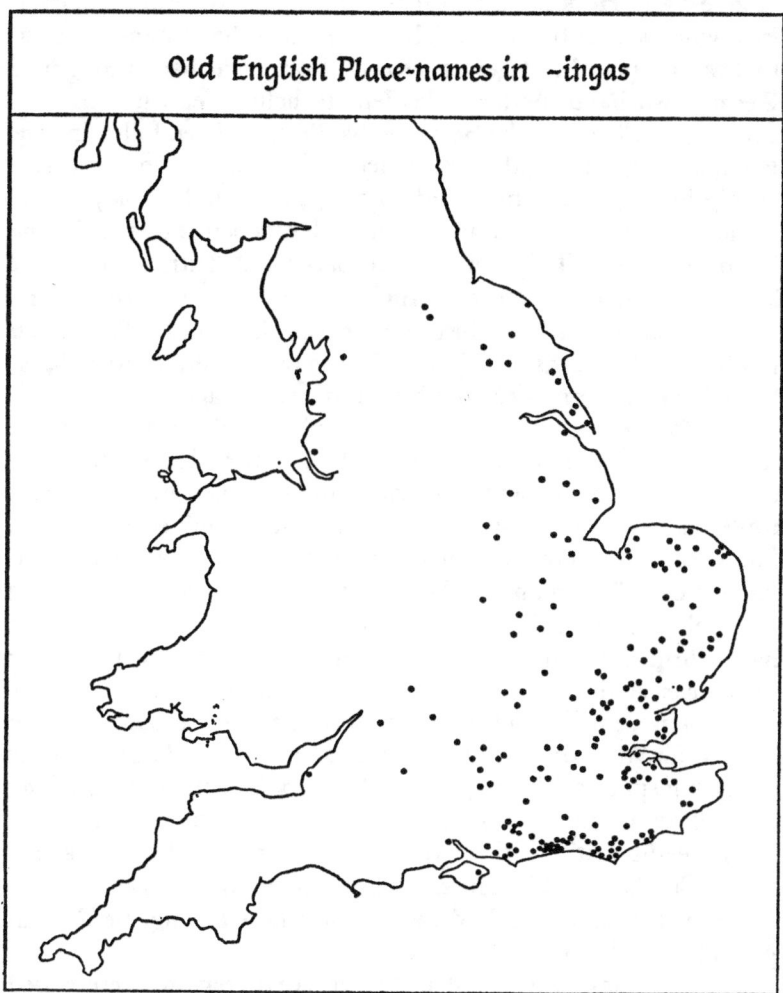

Map 1. See pp. 31-32. Note how these early names are most frequent in the south and east of England.

The Coming of the English

the British', had no success. The stories of Vortigern, Rowena, Hengest and Horsa, are so legendary that one is tempted to overlook whatever truth there might be beneath the romance. Nevertheless, if (as the legends assert) Vortigern had brought a German warband, under its leaders, to help defend his kingdom against the Picts and the Scots, he would have been following the Roman precedent; and if, as the legend continues, the barbarians repaid him by taking his kingdom away, he would be playing out a not improbable drama. It had happened before; it has happened since. This much is probably the truth beneath the legend. From that base the Anglo-Saxons (for such they were) seem to have struck against the British cities and villas. Their raiding, in the words of Gildas, a Briton born half a century later, 'licked the western ocean with its red and savage tongue'.

The foothold gained by Hengest and his followers was of one sort, but there were others. The Anglo-Saxon raiders sailed across the sea to land at various points, and to penetrate by various routes. It was not a planned invasion, with a unified command, but a looser movement, which took a great many years to complete itself. The groans of the British were unanswered near the mid-point of the fifth century. Half a century later, the invaders had a firm hold on the eastern shores of Britain; but there was resistance. Arthur is a legend also; in reality he may not have been a king, but a military commander; but he apparently won battles for the British, and his people won a fairly lengthy breathing space at the beginning of the sixth century. In the long run resistance failed. Gildas, about 540, laments the death of twenty-eight British cities; we may wonder what he took a city to be. But behind his lament there is undoubtedly some truth: urban civilization, as it had been known here during the Roman period, ceased to be.

The eventual relations of British to Anglo-Saxons were raised in Chapter 2, where we noted some of the British place-names which still survive. This is evidence that, in some cases at least, the British retained their language. It is now time to turn to the Anglo-Saxons themselves.

The Anglo-Saxons themselves

They were of various northern European tribes, speaking a common language which became differentiated into various

The Coming of the English

dialects only after the settlement in Britain; they came from various tribal homelands on the Baltic and North Sea coasts; they were probably Angles, Saxons, and Jutes (as the Venerable Bede, the greatest historian before the Conquest, wrote in the eighth century). It is almost impossible to assign a specific continental home to the Jutes who may, in the words of one historian, have been 'made in Kent'. Friesland, in North Holland, was probably an intermediate territory through which the Anglo-Saxons passed on their way westwards. Whether there were amongst the invaders any special group known as Frisians is doubtful, but possible. Certainly there are a number of places which do name them—Freston in Suffolk, Friston in the same county, Frisby in Leicestershire, and others. But these are later names, of the Danish period, when Frisians are more certainly identified. The point remains, however, that Bede may be neither complete nor accurate in his account of the peoples who invaded Britain. It seems too simple a picture to be readily trusted. They were in fact a mixed bunch. There is one tribe well authenticated on English soil which Bede fails to name—the tribe of the Hwicce, which settled mostly on the south-eastern borders of what is now Wales—Glamorgan, Worcestershire and Warwickshire. Whichford, in Warwickshire, is an example of the name: 'the ford of the Hwicce'. Isolated groups of these people presumably split off from the main tribal centre. Wichnor, in Staffordshire; Whiston, in Northamptonshire; and perhaps Hitcham, in Buckinghamshire, have the tribal name in them.

To summarize: a mixed group of tribes started attacking in the fifth century, strengthened their hold in the sixth, and had completed most of their advance by the middle of the seventh. They came into the land by the most usable routes—up the larger rivers such as the Humber, the Trent, and the Thames; in via the Wash. They established themselves first along the south coast and the east, and spread along the valleys into the interior. The pattern of English kingdoms usually called the Heptarchy (though there were certainly more than seven of them at first, and much less than seven later on) had been established by about the year 650. This is the simple historical outline. The two centuries covered by these events must have seen the establishment of a very large number of place-names; no other period can have produced so many. The names themselves help to fill out the details of the invasion and settlement; it is to these we must now turn.

The Coming of the English

The Earliest Place-names [1]

Some place-names belong to the earliest stages of the English language in Britain, others to later stages. The way these names occur on the map can suggest details about the speed and progress of the English settlement. The following paragraphs give some examples of this:

1   One fairly clear indication of early date can be drawn from place-names which refer to the religious practices of Anglo-Saxon paganism, for these would not have originated after the coming of Christianity into the kingdoms where they occur. Names of this sort are considered in a later chapter, but here we may anticipate and give the W. Midlands example of Wednesbury and Wednesfield—sites with a clear connection with the God Woden. The converse of this is of course also true: words with a clear allusion to Christianity do not form place-names of the pagan period.

2   The very common place-name element *ham* belongs largely to the earlier period, though it can also be used in fairly late names. Where an area has a large number of *ham* names, it is very likely to be an area which was settled early in the Anglo-Saxon period. A glance at a map of Kent would show many examples: Chatham, Gillingham, Faversham, Meopham, etc., and there are many also in Sussex and Essex, and in the south and east generally. On the other hand, the equally common place-name element *ton* came into regular use at a later period than *ham*. Its early meaning was 'enclosure'. As a free word, and not a part of place-names, it developed into the modern *town*. At a fairly early stage it came to be a synonym for *ham*, and in the later period of the settlement of the English it came to be used instead of it in the formation of place-names. Names of this sort are frequent in the Midlands and the West, in counties where ham names are rare—Cheshire and Staffordshire are examples. There are only about half a dozen *hams* in Staffordshire, and most of these are obscured by later development in the names. Trentham —the ham on the river Trent—is the clearest. A rough guide to the order in which the various areas of the country were settled

---

[1] The arguments which allow one to judge the relative dates of place-names are subtle. For a penetrating account of them the reader should look at a lecture by A. H. Smith: *Place-names and the Anglo-Saxon Settlement* (British Academy, 1956).

The Coming of the English

is therefore the comparison of *ham* and *ton* names. Putting it roughly: more *hams* than *tons*, early. More *tons* than *hams*, late.

3   There are some words which occasionally occur in place-names in very archaic forms; forms which had probably passed out of use very soon after the coming of the Anglo-Saxons. When these are found in the place-names it is a sure indication of early date. The word *eastor* is one such; Eastrea in Cornwall and Eastry in Kent contain it. It is an early form of the adjective 'eastern', which (as 'east') occurs in Eastwick (Herts) and many others. Another example is the place-name element *ge*, pronounced *yea*, meaning a 'district'. According to A. H. Smith, this is 'found chiefly in the SE, in place-names of great antiquity'. Eastry in Kent has it at the end—a combination of two archaic forms; so has Ely (the eel district); so has Surrey. It will be noticed that this word often survives as a final *y* in a place-name. Perhaps the warning is unnecessary: only a few with the final *y* have this origin. Archaic words and forms in place-names are not as easily spotted as all that!

4   Most attention has been paid by local historians and others to place-names which have the element *ing* as part of them; and these are more readily observed than the features we have just considered. Unfortunately, whilst it is true that many place-names with *ing* in them are very old, it is not true that all of them are. The oldest and most important are those that originally ended in *-ingas*, for these were, in the beginning, *folk*-names rather than *place*-names. Hastings means 'the followers of Haesta'; subsequently it comes to refer to the area in which those followers are settled. Haesta, Reada (of Reading), Angenmaer (of Angmering) and other men so commemorated may have been leaders of warbands, or tribal groups on trek. Names of this sort point to a period before settlement had been consolidated, since people on the move have as yet no territory with which they can be identified. They also record the actual event of settlement: where Hastings now is, there Haesta's folk came to rest. *-Ing* names, however, are tribal names only where the first element is the name of a person. Where it is something else (a topographic or habitation name in itself, for instance) it has often to be interpreted as 'the dwellers at —': for instance, Dorking—the dwellers on the river *Dork (an earlier name for the Mole?). Often, indeed, it may be merely a suffix of a very general meaning, as in Clavering which means a clover field. Professor Smith has shown that names

31

The Coming of the English

of this sort were given all through the Old English period. There is no particular antiquity about them. Other place-names which were originally folk-names are now the names of counties—Essex (the east Saxons); Middlesex (the middle Saxons); Norfolk (the north folk), and so forth.

Later Names

In discussing the chief forms of early Anglo-Saxon names we have noticed the later ones too. Words in *ton*, we said, are usualy late, and found mostly in the counties towards the north and west. Words with elements such as priest, bishop, and monk in them are obviously post-conversion; Preston, Bispham, and Monkton are examples. (Bispham shows, by the way, that *ham* remained a living place-name element until after the conversion at least.)

Names of one element only—monothematic names, as they are called—are also usually late; on the argument that there would have to be an already existing population in the surrounding area before so simple a designation could be a workable name. Examples are: Stowe—'place'; Stoke—'place', or later 'monastery' or 'cell'; Cotes—'cottages'.

Most of the names we have considered in this chapter have been settlement-names—names given from the first to places where people lived. But there are other names: names of woods and fields, fords and hills—which in their first use were not found as habitation-names at all. When later on people expanded out of their first settlements into new houses, it seems to have been normal for the new settlement to take the name of the field or ford or hill on which or by which it was established. But this story—the story of the spread of settlement—is the subject of the next chapter.

Chapter 4
The Spread of Settlement

At the end of Chapter 3 we made a distinction between two sorts of name: habitation-names proper—those which, from the first, were names given to actual Anglo-Saxon settlements; and nature-names; those which referred to places which would probably not have been inhabited in the earliest times, but on which later settlements might come to be placed. In this latter class should be included the names of woods, fields, valleys, and clearings. Of course these later settlements may never be made at all. A good many features of the landscape bear Anglo-Saxon names, and have never been inhabited. Nobody lives on the top of Kinder Scout, but as we said in Chapter 2 the name is Celtic. In this chapter, however, our subject is that of those names which did become places of settlement. It should be apparent that, whilst many such secondary settlements did retain the nature-names of the sites they were founded on, others could have had habitation names in the same way as primary settlements. Often, there may be no clue in the name as to the nature of the settlement, whether primary or secondary. Sometimes on the other hand the name indicates it very clearly indeed. Norton—the North tun—is a tun established to the north of some other place. It is reasonable to suppose that the other place housed the parent community from which Norton was set up.

The spread of settlement took place outwards from the centres of primary settlement. To see how and why this happened requires a brief word about the nature of Anglo-Saxon settlements, and the economic life they existed to further.

Names ending in *ham*, *ing*, and (usually) *ton* were primary settlements. We can imagine the incoming Anglo-Saxons setting up their homes here, and beginning from that time to cultivate the land around them. (They came to some parts of the country earlier than to others; but here we are concerned with the first arrival in any area, whatever its order in the sequence of colonization as a whole.) These settlements were nucleated; that is, the

The Spread of Settlement

houses were clustered together into a community, not scattered over the country-side.

Outside the village was the plough-land on which grains—wheat, oats, barley and rye—were grown. It is generally accepted, though not absolutely provable, that the plough-land was divided into large open fields in which a rotation of crops was practised and that a portion of the land—a third or a half—lay fallow throughout the year to allow it to recover its fertility. This made for stability of settlement since the soil did not become exhausted and so could be tilled indefinitely. This method was, however, wasteful of land because a high proportion gave no yield in a given year. Nevertheless, the open-field system endured for many hundreds of years. Thousands of acres were cultivated in this manner as late as the eighteenth century when wholesale enclosures and re-distribution reduced it to a minimum. There is a surviving example at Laxton in Nottinghamshire which is preserved by the National Trust and which can be inspected by appointment.

The open fields were divided into strips; each villager had a number corresponding to the size of his holding. Ownership of land was not in a single block as in a modern farm, but was scattered over the fields. It is thought that this was to give a rough equality in the varieties of soil, and of access to the fields from the village. Often, though by no means always, these strips were not eliminated when the fields were enclosed in modern times and they can still be identified in a number of places. In Derbyshire, for example, at Chelmorton, Taddington and other places, the strips are enclosed by dry stone walls making an unmistakable pattern on the hillsides. At Appleton-le-Moors, in Yorkshire, strips have been thrown together leaving elongated rectangles surrounded by hedges. Aerial photography has disclosed the remnants of strip cultivation and open fields in many parts of England; Padbury in Buckinghamshire, Brounton in Devonshire and Broxholme in Lincolnshire are a few examples. Indeed, wherever the terms *ton* or *ham* appear in a place-name it is worthwhile to look for the remnants of open fields unless, of course, the surrounding ground is heavily built-up. An invaluable guide to this type of research is *Medieval England* by M. W. Beresford and J. K. S. St Joseph.

As well as growing grain the Anglo-Saxons kept herds of cattle, flocks of sheep and large numbers of pigs. When the grain had

The Spread of Settlement

been gathered these animals were pastured on the open fields where they ate the straw and corn which had fallen in harvesting and also manured the soil with their droppings. During spring and summer while the crops were growing the livestock was turned out to graze in the waste of uncultivated land which divided one village from another. In the early years of the Anglo-Saxon occupation this waste land was very extensive and most of it would be woodland, moor or scrub according to the nature of the soil.

Some of this land would be unsuitable for the plough or difficult to clear, for the best and most easily worked land would be worked first. It is interesting that, in many places, a string of *tons* will follow a line of rich, lighter soil. Pasturing beasts, however, has a beneficial effect on land unless they are so many as to exhaust the herbage. Their manure enriches the soil, their hooves pulverize it and, if they are confined within a corral or enclosure, they prevent the further growth of scrub by treading on the saplings. In the course of years many such glades in the woodland became, by simple pasturing, suitable for cultivation by a little further clearing of timber. The initial clearing was probably done to provide wood for building houses, barns and byres and for firewood.

A clearing in the forest, for pasturing, was called a *leah* by the Anglo-Saxons. This term has given rise to a number of forms —*ley, leigh, lay, ly*. By the time of the *Domesday* record (1086) many places whose name contains one or other of these elements were, as the entry makes it clear, no longer pastures but settlements. Tarporley, in Cheshire, is a good example. The place-name means a glade near a hill in a pear wood. Domesday records seventeen men (and presumably their families) living in Tarporley with about five hundred acres of cultivated land.[1] The metamorphosis from forest glade to village probably took some such form as follows: Clearings and improvement of land coincided with a small but certain growth of population in the centuries immediately following the Anglo-Saxon invasions. The existing ploughland in a given village would be insufficient to maintain a larger number of people. The enlargement of the cultivated area round the village beyond about a thousand acres would be uneconomic and unhandy owing to the distance from the village of the perimeter, for the Anglo-Saxons used oxen for

[1] 4 caracates.

The Spread of Settlement

ploughing and the ox-team moves slowly, more slowly than horses and far more slowly than the modern tractor. It would be necessary to hive-off some of the population from the parent settlement to new land some distance away. Forest glades which had been used for a generation or so as pasture would provide an attractive site. Many nucleated villages were established in them, more particularly in the wooded areas of the Midlands and West. The name which denoted the land's previous use was no longer appropriate but it was retained. Tarporley, the glade where the beasts had pastured, was now a *ton* in everything but name.

Secondary settlements in woods had various names. The terms *wald, wold, holt, shaw, hurst grove* were all used, as well as *wood* itself. Place-names of this character are very common:

HAYWOOD	Wiltshire, Nottinghamshire, Shropshire, Staffordshire. A wood which is also an enclosure
DUNWOOD	Hampshire. A wood on a hill
HOCKERWOOD	Nottinghamshire. A wood on a hump of ground
FULSHAW	Cheshire. A small, boggy wood. (*Ful* is the word 'foul')
BIRCHOLT	Kent. The birch wood
GLEDHOLT	Yorkshire. Wood where there are kites
BROMSGROVE	Worcestershire. Breme's grove
KIDSGROVE	Staffordshire. Cyddi's grove. (These last two names include personal names in them)

Grove sometimes appears as greave, grave, or grieve. It is often joined to the name of a tree, a bird, or an animal:

MUSGRAVE	Westmorland. Mouse wood
RAMSGREAVE	Lancashire. Ram's wood
BOXGRAVE	Sussex. The box-tree wood

Hurst is another term also associated with animal names quite frequently:

BROCKHURST	Wiltshire. This is one of many places which contain the name of the badger—an animal much more common even today than town-dwellers usually realize
CROWHURST	Surrey
DEERHURST	Kent. These last two names explain themselves

COLLYHURST, in Lancashire, is interesting for the glimpse it gives of an Anglo-Saxon occupation—the burning of charcoal for

The Spread of Settlement

use in the smelting of iron. *Colly* means 'coaly'. This does not refer to coal in the modern sense, for although the Anglo-Saxons were excellent smiths, it was not until long after their time that iron came to be smelted with coal. Charcoal was used instead. Great inroads were made in the forests by charcoal burners, and villages grew up in association with the industry, often on the land which had been cleared in the process.

The terms *wald*, *wold*, and *weald* mean 'woodland'—a more general meaning than the specific ones we have just considered. There are Wealds in Sussex, Kent, Hampshire, Oxfordshire and Essex; there is a wield in Hampshire; there are the wolds of Yorkshire, and there are the Cotswolds. In the course of time many of these tracts of land have been cleared of wood and now they generally denote bare open country. Settlements were made in such areas, very often being given a name which has an indication of direction in it; for instance, Northwold in Northumberland, and Southwold in Suffolk. There is also Methwold (middle wold) in Norfolk. Place-names which have directional indications of this sort in them usually denote secondary settlements, even though the other element may be one which can also serve for a primary settlement. *Ton* is one such element. The very common name Norton, as we have said, suggests an offshoot of some older settlement which will probably be found lying to the south of it. Weston would have its parent community to the east, and Sutton to the north. The fourth member of this quartet may occur as Aston, or Eaton, or Easton. It is not quite as reliable an indication as the others, however, as a name of this form can have the alternative origin in 'the tun by the ash tree'. Each case needs separate study. Another -tun name of obvious significance as these is Middleton—a settlement we should expect to find placed between two other settlements. Middlewood in Cheshire is still in the midst of a wood. Then there are the high and low settlements, sometimes also called 'up' or 'down'. Among these are High Ercall in Shropshire, Lowleighton in Derbyshire, Upholland in Lancashire, Downham in Norfolk. There are also the Nethertons, and the Overtons; and Otherton—two of them—one in Staffordshire and one in Worcestershie. Both mean 'the other *ton*', again clearly indicating a secondary settlement.

Newtons are ubiquitous. It is odd to see that, according to the *Domesday* record, they were sufficiently developed to be, by the eleventh century, many hundreds of years old. The term 'old' in

The Spread of Settlement

a place-name is sometimes a trap—the place-name may be comparatively modern, as in Old Sarum in Wiltshire or Old Castle in Cheshire. Old Hurst, Huntingtonshire, mentioned in a document dating from the thirteenth century, is situated near to Woodhurst and both must have been once called Hurst and were later differentiated by calling the original settlement 'old'. Oldmixton in Somerset has an unsavoury connection with a dunghill—the old mixen or midden. Oldberrow in Warwickshire is interesting, an example of the pitfalls that lie in wait for the insufficiently equipped place-names hunter. The berrow is a barrow or ancient burial ground and the first element is a modification of an Anglo-Saxon personal name 'Ulla'. A mile away there is a village called Ullenhall. Evidently, Ulla built a hall which presumably was associated with a village, and was buried nearby after which another village was established near the barrow. Both these villages are mentioned in a document dated AD 709.

The names of animals often appear in place-names, often in association with the term 'wic', which occurs in modern forms of place-names as 'wich' or 'wick'. So, there is Bulwick in Northumberland, and Cowick in Derbyshire and also in the West Riding of Yorkshire. The record of shepherding sheep is preserved in two places called Shapwick (one in Dorset and the other in Somerset) and in another called Shopwyke, in Sussex. It is clear that these places were first names as sites where animals were herded; and that afterwards became settlements for people. This raises the question of the early meaning of the word *wic*—unfortunately, a question which has no easy answer.

The above names might suggest that, among the meanings the word could have, would be that of a hut or isolated building used for a specified occupation. It is striking that a very large number of occurrences of it show it joined to specific nouns, indicating specialized activity:

BEWICK	Northumberland. Honey farm
GOSWICK	Northumberland. Goose farm
SALTWICK	Northumberland. Place where salt was produced. (By evaporating sea-water, very probably)
FISHERWICK	Staffordshire. (FISHWICK, Staffordshire, and also Derbyshire.) Places where fish were obtained. (Freshwater fish, in these cases, because they are inland areas)

The Spread of Settlement

BUTTERWICK   Durham, Lincolnshire, Westmorland, Yorkshire, etc. Butter farm
BERWICK   Very many counties. Barley farm

It is safest to take this as the standard meaning. That names such as EASTWICK and WESTWICK occur suggest, again, secondary settlements. NORTHWICH and MIDDLEWICH are precisely equivalent to the other names embodying directional clues which we have seen. One should suppose that the Anglo-Saxon primary settlement would establish outposts in which these various specialized activities went on. Most of these activities were not the basic agricultural activities of the community; only the words such as Berwick are to do with ploughing and reaping. Most frequent of all, the wicks seem to be connected with the keeping of animals, and especially with dairy-farming.

Near to the centre of Manchester there is a populous district named Ardwick. This was, originally, Ethelred's dairy-farm. (Ethelred was an Anglo-Saxon personal name.) Ardwick is on the banks of a small river, the Medlock. A little further upstream there was another dairy-farm named after Baac, now called Beswick. The Medlock, now a murky ditch, must, long years ago (with its water meadows), have been an eminently suitable place for the keeping of cattle. Barnoldswick, a woollen manufacturing town in Yorkshire, originated as a dairy-farm belonging to Beorwulf.

There is an interesting feature of many of the Cheshire names ending in '-wich'—and of some other names in other counties: they are all places where salt is or has been produced. Nantwich, Northwich and Middlewich, and Droitwich in Worcestershire, are all situated on salt-beds; and in late Anglo-Saxon times they were populous and thriving places.

Salt was very important in Anglo-Saxon economy not only for seasoning but for preserving and curing meat for the winter months. Until comparatively modern times little was known about keeping cattle alive in winter and a slaughtering of all but the breeding stock took place in November. The carcasses of cattle and pigs were salted and laid in pits to supply flesh food until the remaining animals could breed or be fattened on the spring grass.

The production of salt was effected by a process of evaporation. These centres lay above the rock salt, and the wells and springs of the area were impregnated with it; they contained heavily charged brine. This brine was reduced by boiling over wood-fires and the

The Spread of Settlement

resultant sludge was hung in wicker baskets to dry out into salt crystals. Salt was obtained in these places in Roman times and during the Anglo-Saxon period, though documentary evidence for Anglo-Saxon working does not appear until the eleventh century. The Norman Commissioners who compiled the Cheshire entries for the *Domesday* record took some pains to give details of the salt working and its customs and this is not surprising for a tax on salt was an important part of revenue. The following is a translation of part of the entry in the *Domesday Book* for Nantwich:

In the time of King Edward (the Confessor) there was a witch in Nantwich in which was a well for making salt and between the King and the Earl there were eight salt houses so divided that of all their issues the King had two parts and the Earl the third. Besides this the Earl had one salt house at Acton which was his own. From this salt house the Earl had sufficient salt for his house but if he sold any from thence the King had two pence and the Earl one penny for the toll. In the same witch many men from the country had salt houses... In King Edward's time it was worth £21.

We see here evidence of a thriving industry, and it is not surprising that the word *wich* came in later years to have the new meaning of 'salt works' or 'brine spring'. The translator of this extract from *Domesday Book* so used it. It was never used in this specialized meaning in Anglo-Saxon times, however; it gains it a long while afterwards.

To return to discussion of secondary settlements: it does seem reasonable to suppose that place-names which include '-wich' or '-wick' started as specialized buildings or groups of buildings connected with some earlier settlement, and then came to be themselves the centres of secondary settlement.

If one thinks about the nature of some of the activities they commemorate, and other names composed with other elements than wich also, one can see that they might often be such as were best carried on at some distance from the village. The keeping of pigs is one such: they were important in the Anglo-Saxon economy, and they could most conveniently be kept in the extensive forest and woodland which provided acorns and beech-mast, pig-nuts and roots in abundance.

It was only necessary to turn the pigs into the forest and they would find their own food. The pig of Anglo-Saxon times was a much more bony and agile animal than its modern descendant and was only half-domesticated. Boars ran wild in the forests and were hunted for sport and for food. It is probable that the sows were left in the forest until they were heavy in pig and then rounded up into corrals or enclosures. After farrowing and when the piglets wee weaned the herd would be sorted into those who were to be returned to the woodland to breed again and those who were to be killed for pork or salted for bacon. The place-names connected with the herding and breeding of swine occupy more than two columns of close print in Ekwall's Dictionary of English place-names. Some of them can be dated by documents from the eighth century onward. Only a few can be given here:

SWINDEN	Gloucestershire. The pig hill or pig valley
SWINDON	Staffordshire. The pig's hill
SWINEFLEET	Yorkshire. The pig's stream
SWINSTEAD	Lincolnshire. Homestead where pigs were reared
SWINGFIELD	Kent. The pig's field
SWINTON	Lancashire. Pig farm

Swineherds lived in huts in woodland enclosures. They and their families could form the nucleus for a village settlement. When the rearing of pigs was abandoned at one place, because the ground became stale and unwholesome, the land might be cleared and ploughed, and a new village established.

Secondary settlements increased in size, and increased in number, as the population grew larger. They are often found at fords and bridges—places where a few huts might first congregate to cater for the needs of travellers. Our two earliest universities, Oxford and Cambridge, are the obvious examples of this. Oxford is 'the ford where oxen are', or 'the ford where oxen may cross'; it is interesting to remember that the name Bosphorous means precisely the same. The site of Oxford became as the economy developed a very important point for commercial routes.

There is some slight evidence from place-names that fords may occasionally have been in private ownership. Chelford, in Cheshire, was Ceolla's Ford, and 'Ceolla' is a personal name. Bridges were sometimes in private hands too, at a period rather later than the one we are here dealing with.

We have seen how settlements spread out from the primary centres into the woodlands, the pastures, and other suitable places. As time went on land in much less propitious places would be colonized—cultivated, and have homes established on it. Heaths, moors, mosses and fens were gradually settled. At first

The Spread of Settlement

there would be a process of nibbling at the edges, but later settlements would spread more widely over the area. Some of these hard districts were colonized by the Danes and the Norsemen, who will be the subject of a later chapter. There was settlement by the Anglo-Saxons, however.

The difficulties they encountered are often implied by the name. Land on the edge of moors or within them is unrewarding to the farmer. Only by very modern methods can it satisfactorily be ploughed and seeded; it yields very poor pasture. Many thousands of such acres remain untilled in this country down to today. Heaths are slightly better, though the land is usually poor, light and dry; the farmers call it 'thirsty'. Marsh and fenlands offer opposite difficulties; here there is too much water near the surface. Heavy clay is also difficult. If lime is used to break up its close texture, it can become rewarding, but it is very unlikely that the Anglo-Saxons used it to any appreciable extent. How could it be transported except at enormous cost in time and labour from the lime districts to the clay districts?

In spite of all these difficulties, Anglo-Saxon settlements are found on these difficult soils. They are mostly isolated farms and hamlets, but there are some larger centres too. They were established late in the Anglo-Saxon period, in most cases. They cannot generally be dated earlier than the Conquest and their first record is normally in the Domesday Book. Here are a few examples:

CLAYTON-LE-MOOR	Lancashire. The place-name describes a combination of difficulties for this ton—clay and moorland
CLAYDON BOTOLPH	Oxfordshire. The house on clay
MORESTEAD	Hampshire. The place by a moor or fen
MORE	Shropshire
FENCOTE	Herefordshire. Cottages in a fen
FENTON	Cumberland. Ton by a fen
HEATHCOTE	Derbyshire. The cottage on the heath
HEATON	There are many of these scattered over the country. They are often composite names, for example, Heaton Norris, Lancashire, and Hanging Heaton, Yorkshire. 'Hanging' means 'high'
MOSTON	Cheshire. Ton by the moss
MOSSBROUGH	Derbyshire. The fortified place in a moss
MOSS-SIDE	Lancashire

Chapter 5
Religion and Superstition

St Augustine and his fellow missionaries arrived in England in the year 597. The attractive story of how Gregory, before he became pope, came upon some English slaves, is well known. On being told that they were Angles, he replied: 'Non Angli, sed Angeli'—not Angles, but Angels. On hearing that they were from the country of Deira (the southern part of the kingdom of Northumbria), he supposed that they were so called because they were saved from wrath—*de ira*—and called to the mercy of Christ. The third of his solemn puns concerned the name of their king, Aelle—the first two syllables, he observed, of the word 'Allelujah'. The story is told by the venerable Bede, in the history of the English Church, which he wrote just over a century after Augustine's arrival. The conversion of England obviously did not depend solely upon this accidental meeting in the market-place; the story is merely a charming ornament to the event. Roman missions to England would not have been delayed very long in any case.

Christianity was not new to Britain. Much earlier, it had made its way amongst the Romano-British, in the later stages of the Roman occupation; and it had survived the final departure of the Roman legions in the early fifth century. During the years of Diocletian's persecution (beginning in AD 303) there were a few British martyrs, and the name of one of them has survived in St Pancras, where he is commemorated by the name of a district of North London and the important railway terminus there. In the fourth century Christianity in Britain was sufficiently important to produce its own heresy, advanced by Pelagius, a monk and theologian. There are records of British monasteries, and of British bishops attending synods in Gaul. In the period after the withdrawal of Roman armies, two figures stand out: St Patrick, who took Christianity from Britain to Ireland in 431, and the monk Gildas, who wrote in about 540 a bitter lament for the

Religion and Superstition

desolation which had come upon the land with the defeats of his people at the hands of the Anglo-Saxons. By his time, the Welsh Church was firmly established. One might have thought that when the fighting died down there would have been some missionary activity directed towards the Anglo-Saxons from this Church in Wales. This did not happen, however. Memories were too bitter. The exclusiveness of the Welsh Christians remained a problem for many years. But the Irish Church which St Patrick had established saw things differently. From Ireland, missions were set up in Scotland; and from Scotland, missionaries came into Northumbria, where there was an important centre on the island monastery of Lindisfarne.

When St Augustine arrived in the south of England from Rome, Irish missionaries were already at work in the north. Christianity was also known in the south. Ethelbert the king of Kent, and the overlord of the whole of the southern part of England, had a Christian wife, and she had her private bishop. She was a Frankish princess, Bertha by name, the daughter of the king of Paris.

There was for a while competition between the Celtic and Roman Churches. They differed in many matters of practice, for the Celtic Church had become isolated from the main body of Mediterranean Christianity before Rome came to assert the primacy which made its Bishop the leader of the Catholic Church as a whole. The tension and rivalry between the churches was settled at the Synod of Whitby in 664, where the decision was taken for the English Christians to adhere to the Roman practices; and the Celtic Church in England was eclipsed—leaving behind, however, a tradition of saintliness and learning which was of permanent importance.

It would be valuable if we could know whether any given place were a centre of Celtic or Roman Christianity, in this period of rivalry between the Churches. Dedications to Celtic saints are perhaps one indication: Chadkirk, in Cheshire, refers to a church of St Chad, for instance. Beyond this, there is the evidence of place-names which derive from the British (Celtic) word *eclesia*, which means a church and which is itself taken from Greek. It was used in the Christian community in the very early years of its existence. The use of this word as an element in English place-names does not guarantee that there was a British church on the site, but it is at least a fairly broad hint of it. If the area in which

Religion and Superstition

it is found lies close to where clear Celtic place-names occur, indicating the survival of a British community; if there is in the place a church dedication to a Celtic saint; and if the church building is mentioned in *Domesday Book* (being therefore established before 1086) we are on fairly firm ground.

In place-names, the word occurs usually as *eccles*. It is often combined with English elements, and it is found frequently though not exclusively in the north-west midlands. There are places called Eccles in Lancashire and Norfolk; there is Ecclesfield in Yorkshire West Riding; Eccleston in Cheshire; Eccleshall in Staffordshire; and Exley also in Yorkshire.

The rivalry between the Roman and Celtic Churches was enacted against the background of the conversion of the Anglo-Saxons to Christianity, which was a fairly steady progress moving ahead with the conversion of princes and kings first, and of their subjects as a consequence, in the various kingdoms of the English. Where the ruler went, the people followed. The progress was held up where there was an obdurate pagan on the throne. Such a one was King Penda of Mercia. There were occasional reversions; but usually the conversion went smoothly. There were no martyrs.

To complete the story, we must notice that the encounter of Christianity with paganism was altogether more bitter and bloody in the periods of Danish attack which came later. Today we may find it hard to imagine a state in which the churches of the country have to be defended with the sword; in which minsters were systematically despoiled by the heathen. But this was the situation during the various phases of Norse attack.

To read such comments as those of Alfred on the state of learning in England; or of Bishop Wulfstan, in a powerful sermon preached a century and a half later, is to realize vividly how close the enemy was, repeatedly, over a long stretch of time. From time to time, sometimes as part of a peace treaty, the enemy accepted baptism; in the long run, the danger passed. The nature of the Anglo-Saxons' Christianity in this second phase—the phase of conflict with the Danes—is something different from anything known subsequently: churches have not been systematically burned since the Viking invasion.

We may now return to the beginning of the story, and look at the evidence of place-names. The question arises first, from what beliefs and practices were the Anglo-Saxons converted by the Roman and Irish missions of the late sixth and seventh centuries?

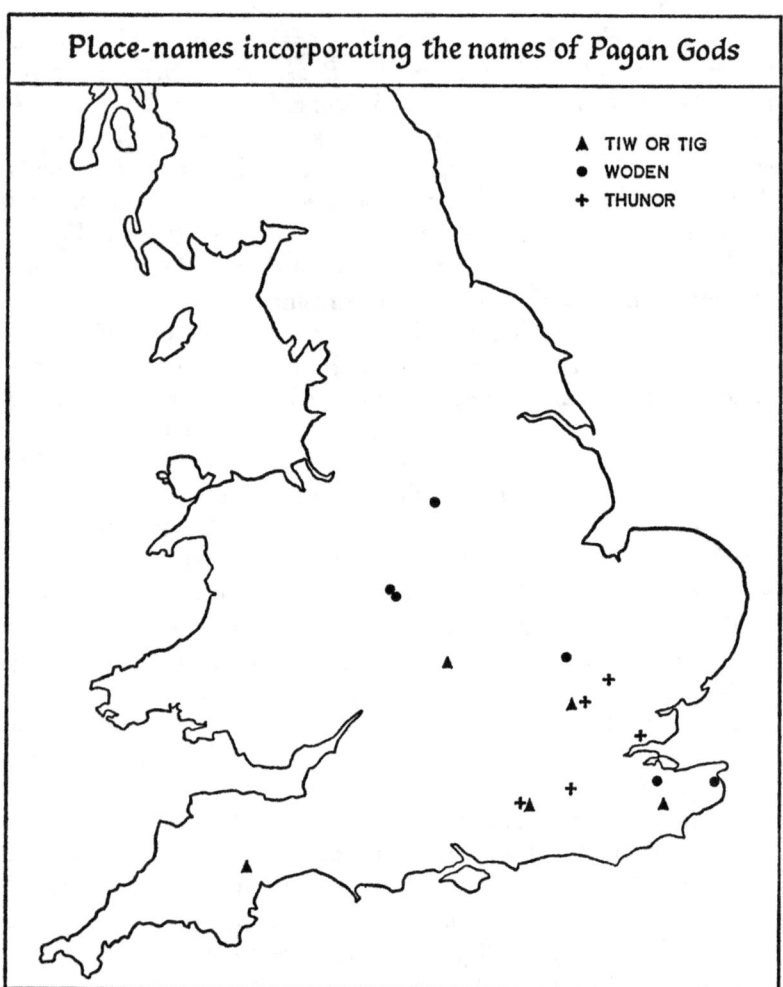

Map 2.   See discussion on pp. 49-50.

We can hardly expect any written evidence of this dating from the days when the pre-Christian practices were in their full vigour, for literacy itself is one of the main accomplishments that Christianity brought with it. There is some indication in later literature. The Old English poem of Beowulf is a valuable source from which to gain an impression of the legends the Anglo-Saxons brought with them from their continental homelands, for instance; there are also charms which have importance as evidence of superstitious practices. But from what these sources tell us, transmitted as they are through Christian scribes and copyists, amongst the pagan English there was no highly developed cult system. There was a code of behaviour—the heroic code, as it is called—which in many respects survived the conversion, but of the gods, and of what stories there may have been about the gods told on English soil, we know nothing. (There is of course a good deal of evidence in later Scandinavian literature; but it is probably not directly applicable to the English scene.) The clues in the names of places are perhaps the best we have; and the next section of this chapter looks at them.

Superstition is something different from religion. Almost all peoples have beliefs in ghosts, hobgoblins, giants and monsters, which persist alongside the more developed religious ideas they may accept. Superstitions are perhaps survivals of earlier, more developed, cults; perhaps they are merely the consequence of fireside spine-chillers, believed in because they make life more interesting. Wherever it comes from, many place-names bear witness to the existence of superstition, and we have no grounds for supposing it to be more appropriate to the pagan stage of Anglo-Saxon history than to the Christian.

Places of Pagan Worship

We may start with the evidence in place-names of actual pagan religious practices. There are a number of words which help us: *hearg*, or *haerg*—this word is one of a small group which means 'a heathen temple'; others are *hof* (Old English and Old Norse); *alh*; and a possible **elgr* (Norse). Names including these words are:

Arrowfield, Worcestershire
Harrowden, Bedfordshire

Religion and Superstition

Harrow-on-the-Hill
Peper Harrow
Hoff, Westmorland
Alkham, Kent
Elloughton, Yorks

(Hoff, heathen temple, may be an old Norse name—the word was the same in both languages.) These examples are scattered widely enough for it to be clear that the pagan English were not without religion of some sort.

The word *weoh*, or *wig*, had the meaning of an idol, or shrine; and there are various places called Weedon (usually meaning 'shrine on the hill') and Weeford (the shrine by the ford). Others are Whyly (Sussex); Willey (Surrey) and Wyeville (Lancashire). The word *heathen* itself is evidently a direct reference to paganism, presumably incorporated into names by the converted English; Heathens' Burial Corner, in Sussex, is nicely informative. Eaton Thorn in Surrey, and Haven Street in the Isle of Wight, are others. (The last example is of popular etymology, in which a word or name is altered to make it more like some more familiar word it is thought to be a version of. In 1339 this road, built by heathens, was written la Hethene Stret.)

Most religions prescribe ways of disposing of the dead. We know that the Anglo-Saxons made use of burial mounds, though many earlier people had done so too, and the tumuli found so frequently on high places of England are as likely to date from very much earlier than the Anglo-Saxons as not. They were known as *hlaws*—a word which gives us the modern *low*, and of which we shall say more below—or as *byrgels*, meaning 'burial place'. This last is sometimes combined with 'heathen', to give a very clear indication indeed: Heathens' Burial Corner, already quoted, is one example. Brailes in Warwickshire, Brailsford in Derbyshire, and Brailsham in Sussex include versions of this word.

Cremation was practised in Early England: we know this from the use of the word bæl, or bel, which means *pyre*.

Belstead in Essex was 'the place of the pyre'; Belgrave, Leicestershire, was 'the grove of the pyre'; there are many places called Belton—the ton by the pyre.

Religion and Superstition

The Names of the Pagan Gods

Tuesday, Wednesday, Thursday and Friday—four of the Germanic gods have given their names to the days of the week; and these are the four that are represented in English place-names too: Tiw, Woden, Thunor, and Frig. The Scandinavian names for these divinities are slightly different; Woden, for instance, was Othinn; and Tiw (who could occur in English as Tig) was in Norse Tyr. Sometimes in north-country place-names it is probably the Scandinavian form we are dealing with; and this means that the date of the place-name is rather later than if it had been originally English. (Sometimes, on the other hand, an English name incorporating one of the gods' names may have been Scandinavianized by the Danes; in which case it is still a pre-conversion example.) Frig, by the way, was a goddess, the consort of Woden. Woden himself sometimes masquerades as Grim: a name which in fact really meant 'a mask', to begin with. Examples of place-names alluding to the pagan gods are:

WODEN	Wansdyke	Woden's Dyke. Compare this with Grimsdyke
	Wednesfield	Staffs. Woden's field
	Wednesbury	Staffs. Woden's fortress
	Wenslow	Beds. Woden's mound
	Woodnesborough	Kent. As Wednesbury
TIW	Tysoe	Warwicks. Tiw's hoh—a space of land
	Tuerley	Surrey. Meadow dedicated to Tiw
THUNOR or THOR	Thundersfield	Surrey. Field dedicated to Thunor or Thor
	Thundersley	Herts. Field dedicated to Thunor or Thor
	Thursley	Surrey. Field dedicated to Thunor or Thor
	Thundridge	Herts. Ridge dedicated to Thunor or Thor
FRIG	Fryup	N. Yorks. Small valley sacred to Frig
	Froyle	Hants. Hill sacred to Frig

49

Religion and Superstition

	Freefolk	Hants. Frig's people (?)
	Fretherne	Glam. Frig's thornbush
GRIM	Grimsbury	Oxford. Grim's fortress
(alias WODEN)		

A. H. Smith notes that the *Thunor* names are confined to what were the Saxon areas of England; this perhaps suggests that the cult of Thor was characteristic of the Saxons. There is also a striking concentration of *Woden* names in the west midlands. Finally, it should be noticed that, since there was a Danish personal name Grim, it is hard to know where the reference is to god and where to a mere mortal. *Grimsby* is an example of the latter (Lincolnshire). *Grimsbury* is a reasonably certain example of the former (Oxfordshire).

Giants and dragons

After the conversion, the old gods lost their hold; but the much more local, less systematic and theological beliefs in giants, and dragons, hobgoblins, and elves, persisted; indeed, there may still be some backward areas of Britain where they persist yet. One or two of the names we shall discuss are fairly new, dating from the Middle English period.

Where a place-name contains such an element as, for instance, *grima*, meaning a spectre, or goblin (the more general word, of which Woden's nickname was a special application), one presumes that it was not a centre of primary habitation. You don't choose to live on a haunted site. Probably all the names discussed in this section were, in the first place, names of hills, or woods, or fields. Settlements, if they came at all, would come later. Three examples containing *grima* illustrate this rather neatly : Greenacre, in Kent, was originally the name of a field (aecer). It is incidentally another name on which popular etymology has been at work. The same is true of Greenhill, in Worcestershire (Grimeshyll in 806)—the name of a hill; and, nearby, at Grimley, we have the name of another wood, this time with the *grima* etymology less concealed.

Our ancestors had a very large number of words for mysterious monsters of various kinds, which are now hard to differentiate. There were, for instance, elves, hobs, bugs, pooks, and, in the Danelaw, even trolls. This is not to include straightforward giants

Religion and Superstition

and dragons, nor at least two varieties of water-spirits. We illustrate some of these names:

Aelf—an elf   Alvden (Lancs), the elf valley, Elva Hill (Cumberland), Elveden (Suffolk)

There was also an Old English word 'elfet', a swan, which could easily be confused with elf; Ekwall's Dictionary, for instance, takes Elveden as meaning 'Swan valley', whilst Smith's English Place-name Elements assumes 'elf valley'. Furthermore, the element 'Elv-' at the beginning of a place-name does not always imply either an elf or a swan; for a number of personal names have become reduced to this in course of time. Alveston in Warwickshire, for instance, was Eanulfestun in 996; the name in question here is that of Eanwulf. The town of the same name in Glamorgan is 'Alwih's stone'.

Puca—an Old English word from which are descended the words *puck* and *pook*. Puckeridge, in Hertfordshire—the goblin stream (the second part of this name is doubtful; it is not the apparent 'ridge'). Parkwalls, Cornwall; Pock Field, in Cambridgeshire; Purbrook, in Hampshire.

Scucca—an evil spirit or demon. Two examples connect this word with *hill*—Shucknall, in Herefordshire; and Shacklow, in Derbyshire. This last includes the word *hlaw*, with the meaning of tumulus or burial mound; evidence that these features were the focus of superstitions. Other examples: Shugborough, Staffs; Scugdale (two examples in north Yorkshire), the valley of the demons; Shocklach, in Cheshire (the demon's stream). The Scandinavian *troll* figures in one place-name in the area of Danish settlement—Troughburn, in Northumberland. The Scandinavians had goblins as well; the name for one was *skratti*, which is to be found in a number of north-country place-names such as Scarthing Moor in Norfolk, Scratters in East Yorkshire, Scratgate in Cumberland.

Two Middle English goblin names figure in place-names also; *bugge* (the modern dialect word boggart) and *hob*, which combines in the word hobgoblin. This is in origin a pet form of the personal name Robin; but how it came to be applied to supernatural creatures it is hard to say. Place-names illustrating these words are:

Bugley in Wiltshire
Buglawton in Cheshire

Religion and Superstition
Hobmoor Lane, Warwickshire
Boggart Hole Clough in Lancashire

The goblins discussed so far are all, perhaps, general-purpose spirits; but our ancestors had also a variety of more specialized monsters; water-spirits; and phantoms. There are two words for 'water-spirit'—a *fifel*, and *nicor*. Fifel occurs in Filey, Yorkshire; and nicor, according to Smith, in a number of field-names. A word for spectre or phantom was *scinna*, which is to be found in Shincliffe, in Durham, and in Skinburness in Cumberland. A magician who raised spectres was a *scinnere*; and one such was perhaps to be found in Shearston, Devon.

The Old English word for witch, from which the word hag is descended, was *haegtesse*. Hascombe in Surrey was 'the witch's valley'; Hescombe in Somerset is the same; Hessenford in Cornwall was the ford of the witches. The west-country connections of these words are interesting. Two words for 'giant' need mentioning—*ent*, and *thyrs*, with its Norse variant *thurs*. Ent occurs in Indescombe, Devon; giant's valley. *Thyrs* occurs in Thrusford, Norfolk; Tusmore, Oxfordshire (a lake—mere—not a moor, as the modern form of the name suggests), Thirlspot (giant's pit) in Cumberland, and Trusey in east Yorkshire; and the Norse form of *thyrs* lies behind Thrushgill in Lancashire. Finally, there are dragons. Typically, in legend, the dragons guard treasure; there is one such in the poem of Beowulf. The treasure is often thought of as the burial goods of some king or rich man, and we know indeed from the Sutton Hoo treasure, discovered in 1939, that the pagan English had the practice of burying with their illustrious dead goods of great beauty and value. Treasure was associated with lonely burial mounds; and such mounds, or *hlaws*, would often have attendant dragons. The three things go together.

The word for dragon is either *wurm* or *draca* (as in *firedrake*); a word for treasure is *hord*; and words for tumulus and hill have already been given. Various combinations of these elements figure in place-names:

DRAKEDALE	Yorkshire north. Dragon's valley
DRAKEHILL	Surrey. Dragon's hill
DRAKELOW	Derbyshire. Burial mound guarded by a dragon

(There is another Drakelow in Worcestershire)

DRAGLEY	Lancashire. Like Drakelow

Religion and Superstition

HURDLOW	Derbyshire. 'Low' containing a treasure hoard
WENSLOW	Bedfordshire. Woden's 'low'
WORMHILL	Derbyshire. Dragon hill
WORMINGHALL	Berkshire. Dragon hollow
WORMWOOD SCRUBBS	Wood frequented by a dragon

Chapter 6
The Coming of the Vikings

Vikings, Norsemen, Northmen, Scandinavians, Danes, the Heathen—these are the rather loose terms for the people who, in the Middle Ages, inhabited the countries which are now Norway, Sweden and Denmark. They were farmers and fishermen, tilling the small patches of fertile land in the creeks and fiords with which their countries were intersected, keeping sheep and cattle on the mountains and taking to the sea in the slack period between seed-time and harvest. From pre-historic times, when they first occupied their homeland, they had been marauders and pirates but, until the end of the eighth century, their activities had been confined to the shores of the Baltic. For reasons which have not yet been fully explained, from the eighth to the eleventh centuries a burst of national energy took these people to all the shores of Western Europe, to the British Isles, to the Shetlands and Orkney, to Greenland and, long before Columbus, to the then unknown continent of North America. Vikings established the first kingdom of Russia; and Viking inscriptions have been found in the Arabian desert. It has been suggested that an amelioration of climate, followed by a population explosion which the available land was insufficient to feed, forced the landless young men to seek new homes. The Vikings were traders as well as pirates; they took when they could and traded when they must.

In the eighth century England had been secure from invasion for two hundred years. A small but significant trade had developed with the continent of Europe. Peaceful traders were an accustomed sight in the ports. In 787, three strange ships were sighted off the coast of Dorset. They were long and square-rigged, perhaps manned by a couple of hundred men, who were at once fighters and rowers. Along the bulwarks the round arm-shields of the pirates were hung, making a characteristic pattern. As the ships approached Wareham, the King's reeve went down to the

The Coming of the Vikings

shore to ask their business and collect the customary dues. He was killed out of hand, the town was sacked and burnt and the Vikings put hastily out to sea taking the loot from the town with them. This first raid was followed by a series of dreadful ravages which grew in severity. In 793 a much larger force landed in Northumberland and sacked a monastery on Lindisfarne, taking away with them much treasure and many illuminated manuscripts. The Scandinavians were heathen, worshipping Thor and Odin; they had no regard for the sanctity of the Christian Church. No monastery or town, especially if it were near to the coast, was safe from destruction.

At first the raids were 'smash and grab' and the raiders returned home with their loot. Later they made settlements from which they could not be dislodged. The entry for the year 851 in the *Anglo-Saxon Chronicle* records:

In this year Ealdorman Ceorl with the men of Devon fought against the heathen ... and made great slaughter and won the victory. And this same year King Athelstan and Ealdorman Ealhhere destroyed a great host at Sandwich in Kent, captured nine ships and drove off the rest. And the heathen for the first time remained over the winter.

This is only one of many entries which describe unavailing efforts to prevent permanent settlement by the Vikings. Fortifying themselves in strongholds they remained in increasing numbers. At this time England was divided into several kingdoms of which the most powerful was Wessex. Wessex was the nucleus of resistance to the Scandinavian invasions, but even Wessex was almost overwhelmed. In Mercia, East Anglia and Northumbria —kingdoms to the north of Wessex—most of the towns and villages were looted and burnt, the monasteries destroyed and the monks slain or scattered. With them was lost much of the wealth and learning which had been painfully gained in the two centuries since the conversion to Christianity. Trade diminished to a trickle. The land was impoverished. There was no central authority to cover the whole country which could organize a national resistance. There was no navy to prevent the landings of the pirate hordes.

In 866, the Viking bands formed themselves into a great confederacy, called 'The Great Army'. This Army fell on England, no longer only for plunder but in order to conquer and occupy the land. They overran the north of England, defeated the

The Coming of the Vikings

Northumbrians at York and sacked the city. They then divided the land among themselves, making thralls of the English, displacing them from their homes and also making new settlements. Much the same sort of thing happened in Eastern Mercia and in East Anglia though not quite to the same extent. Scandinavian place-names are most numerous in Yorkshire; there are many, but not *as* many in the Eastern Midlands and East Anglia. The Viking conquest of East Anglia was marked by a particularly barbarous act, which is commemorated by a place-name—Bury St Edmund. Edmund was King of East Anglia. He fought and lost a great battle with the Viking host and was taken prisoner by their leader, Jarl Ingwar. Ingwar offered Edmund his life on condition that he would forsake the Christian religion, do homage to Ingwar and worship heathen gods. Edmund refused. He was tied to a stake and shot to death by a storm of arrows. His body was secretly buried by his followers and, later, a shrine was raised over it. Later still the great abbey of Bury St. Edmunds was founded and gave its name to a town which grew around the Abbey.

The Scandinavians took three main routes in their piratical voyages from their homeland. One, taken by the Swedes, ran across Russia and reached Constantinople. This does not concern us here. The second route was directly across the North Sea, taken mainly by the Danes. Some of the effects of this invasion have been described; it was the largest in numbers and resulted in the greatest displacement of people. We shall look at it in greater detail shortly. The third route was more complicated. Settlements of Norsemen were made on the north coast of Scotland, in the Hebrides and on the Isle of Man. From these bases Ireland was overrun and Dublin founded. From Dublin, Viking bands raided the estuaries of the Lancashire and Westmorland coasts thus invading England from the west where they were least expected. They left a trail of rapine, destruction and famine behind them. In the eighth, ninth and tenth centuries, Norse settlements were established in the river valleys and coastal plains of Lancashire and Cheshire and in the dales of the Lake District.

At this time the north-western parts of England were very thinly populated. Anglo-Saxon colonization had been sparse and there seem to have been some surviving Celtic people, mainly living in the hills and moorlands. Generally speaking, the Norse settlements were interspersed among the existing rather thinly

The Coming of the Vikings

spread villages already established or else founded on unoccupied land. This is particularly true of the Lake District where the place-names are preponderously Norwegian. Judging by the remains of hut circles and dolmens, the Celtic people continued to live on the shoulders of the lakeland fells and perhaps acted as shepherds for the Norse farmers in the dales.

The question arises at this point as to whether there are any certain ways of distinguishing the areas of Norwegian settlement from those of the Danes, on the evidence of place-names. There are a few indications, though as the languages were really very much alike—dialects not very far developed away from each other—they are slight. 'Thorp' is a place-name element which is characteristic of Danish areas, and rare in Norwegian areas. It means 'a secondary settlement'. Danthorpe, in East Yorkshire, is a convenient name to remember; 'the thorp of the Danes', but there is no example of Normanthorp, which would mean the thorp of the Norwegians. Other Danish examples are: Littlethorp, Grassthorpe, Moorthorpe, Middlethorpe, etc.

Characteristically Norwegian are the elements *gil* (as in Blagill; Reagill; Garrigill), which means 'a narrow valley'; and *brekka*, which means 'a hill' or 'a slope', as in Breck, Warbreck, Scarisbrick, and others. A distinction which would have been useful, had it not been obscured by the later Anglo-Norman habit of spelling 'u' as 'o', in the neighbourhood of 'm' or 'n', is that between *hulm* (Danish) and *holmr* (Norwegian)—variants of a word meaning 'island', or 'water-meadow'. Upper Hulme in Staffordshire is Danish; Oxenholme in Westmorland is Norwegian. But this distinction is a risky one to apply.

The features distinguishing Norwegian from Danish are small compared with those which distinguish Scandinavian names in general from English; though, even here, the languages are closely related, and it would have been easily possible for a Viking to recognize (in a strange pronunciation, one must grant) words in English that were basically the same as those in his own tongue. The various changes which had differentiated the two languages as they developed out of common Germanic, the ancestral language of both of them, left certain parallels. One, which is fairly easy to recognize, is a correspondence between Scandinavian 'k-' or 'sk-' sounds, and English 'ch-' or 'sh-'. The words skirt and shirt are 'doublets', as they are called; and so are church and kirk, birch and birk, and many others. Both English and

The Coming of the Vikings

Map 3. See p. 61. Apart from Tenby, in S. Wales, these places (all those in the AA Handbook ending in -by) lie north and east of a line between the estuaries of the Thames and the Dee.

The Coming of the Vikings

Scandinavians seem to have seen this quite clearly, for there are many cases where a name in the one language is assimilated to the sounds of the other by switching these pronunciations. Kirton, for instance, is a Scandinavianized version of Church-ton (Chirchetune in Domesday); a name which would have normally developed into Cheriton. Kirkstead in Lincolnshire is another example. Keswick is a Norse adaptation of *cesewic*, or 'cheese farm'. (Compare this with Chiswick, in the non-Scandinavian part of the country.)

Names in which existing elements in one language have been assimilated to the pronunciation of the other are frequent. There are also many hybrids where the name is composed of elements taken from separate languages. These most often have the addition of an English sound element to a Scandinavian personal name; names of this type are called 'Grimston hybrids', from a very common example of the process. They point fairly clearly to a genuine mixture of populations. Urmston and Flixton, both in Lancashire, are two further examples.

To return to the historical events of the Norse invasions. We have noticed so far the sporadic attacks by marauding bands, mainly in the north and east of England. In 871, the Viking Great Army, many thousands strong, invaded Wessex. This was a Danish army, made up of Scandinavians who had followed what we have called the second route out of this homeland—directly across the North Sea. In the war with Wessex, no less than six battles were fought in a single year. The King of Wessex, Aethelred, received a mortal wound in a skirmish. The Vikings were defeated in battle but retired to a strongly stockaded camp at Reading and from this they could not be dislodged. Aethelred's younger brother, Alfred, succeeded and in him and his son and daughter the solution to the Viking menace was found. It was not possible to expel the invaders. Their policy of fighting battles at widely separated points coupled with retirement to fortified camps was all too effective against the slower-moving English fyrd (militia) whose members were taken from the plough and byre and who fought on foot.

It is true that the Viking host also fought on foot though, as they penetrated farther and farther inland from their bases on the coasts, they mounted themselves for transit on horses stolen from the English farms. Thus they could strike unexpectedly and, if defeated retreat with speed, only to strike again in another

The Coming of the Vikings

place. So successful were these tactics that Alfred was driven at one stage to take refuge almost alone in a marsh in Somerset. This was the scene of the well-known but improbable story of Alfred and the burnt cakes. Nevertheless, although it seemed at this time that there was no force in all England sufficient to prevent a complete conquest by the invaders, the turning point was at hand. Although not expelled, in the ninth century the Vikings were, so to speak, domesticated—assimilated into national life, eventually becoming part of the English nation.

The story of how this was accomplished is too long to tell in detail here; it can be read in history books. For our purposes two aspects of the assimilation are important for they have had great effects on place-names, both in their character and in their distribution. While Alfred was in hiding in Somerset the Vikings ranged and ravaged all over Wessex. Their leader King Guthrum settled down in a fortified camp at Chippenham, Wiltshire. The men of Wessex, however, rallied and, led by Alfred who emerged from his retreat, made a desperate and successful assault on Guthrum and the main body of his army. The Vikings were driven back to their stockade at Chippenham, blockaded and forced to surrender by starvation. A treaty was made whereby England was divided into two halves, one of which was to be occupied and ruled by the Scandinavian people and the other by the English.

The Danelaw, as it was called, comprised part of what is now Northumberland, all Yorkshire and East Anglia and, roughly the Midlands east of Watling Street (now the A5). South and west of the Danelaw was English territory. The various branches of the Scandinavian people who settled in the Danelaw came to be called, collectively, Danes. Led by King Guthrum, they became Christian, accepted baptism and retired from Wessex. Some of Guthrum's followers, roving spirits who were not attracted to a settled life, went off to continue raiding on the continent of Europe but the majority went from Wessex to found new homes and farms in the agreed territory. Thus, there are no settlement place-names of Scandinavian origin in the south and west of England from this period, though a handful remain from the later eleventh-century invasion under King Canute. These will be dealt with later.

Danish rule in north-eastern England was comparatively mild after the conversion to Christianity. Both people now had the

The Coming of the Vikings

same religion and shared a common worship. The sacking of churches and monasteries soon ceased. The economy and way of life of English and Dane had little differences, though, owing to the character of the territory, Danish farming had a greater emphasis upon animal husbandry than upon arable. This was also true however of the Anglo-Saxons in districts where grain-growing was not easy. The Danes continued the practice, brought with them from Scandinavia, of housing their cattle on the hills and fells during the summer months in temporary shelters called 'booths'. This results in a place-name found repeatedly in what was once the Danelaw. Upper and Nether Booth in Derbyshire, Boothby in Lincolnshire, Bootham in Yorkshire and Crawshawbooth in Lancashire are examples. There are many more. Another Scandinavian word for a booth or shieling was *sætr*, which occurs as 'seat' in such names as Summerseat, Lancashire. A variant is Summerhouse, the name of a place in Durham.

It will have been noticed that most of the Scandinavian place-names discussed above have been adapted from descriptive or occupational uses. Of names which are purely settlement-names, the most frequent and by far the most important element they may contain is the *by*. It is found all over what was the Danelaw, as well as in the north-west. Travelling along the A5, the old Watling Street, one notices that the sign-posts bristle with names with this ending. They point to places on both sides of the dividing line, showing that there was some Danish infiltration across it; but they are much more plentiful on the eastern side of the road. The element is found particularly in Yorkshire. It is less numerous in East Anglia, and found still less frequently in the north-west. It is not found at all south and west of London. It can be seen that the number of names ending in *-by* in an area is a good indication of the density and distribution of Scandinavian settlement. (See map on p. 58.)

The word means a farmhouse or a village. Many farmhouses became the nuclei of subsequent villages, and it is therefore not always possible to determine which meaning was intended at the naming of any given place. It is likely, though, that many 'bys' were named as communal settlements, rather than as single farms, after the peace treaty between Alfred and the Danes. A large number of them have personal names or nicknames as their first elements. (The Scandinavians were greatly given to nicknames: Ivar the Boneless, Harald Harefoot, Harald Blue-Tooth and Eric

The Coming of the Vikings

Blood-Axe are names which enliven some rather desperate chapters of history.) The following are 'bys' formed with personal names:

Yorkshire
AINDERBY   Eindrioi's village. (Eindrioi means 'the supreme ruler')
HELPERBY   Hialp's village. (A woman's name)
SCALBY   Skalli's village. (*Skalli* is a nickname meaning 'skull')
UNCLEBY   Hunchil's village. (Popular etymology; see chapter 8)
SLINGSBY   Sleng's village. (*Sleng* is a nickname meaning 'idler')
UGGLEBARNBY   Uglubaroi's village. (A nickname meaning 'owl')
FLASHBY   Flatr's village
HELLABY   Helgi's village

Lancashire
FORMBY   Forni's village (A very common personal name)

Lincoln
GRIMSBY   Grim's village. (Another common personal name. 'One who wears a mask')
HACONBY   Hacun's village

Norfolk
ALBY   Alli's village
MAUTBY   Malti's village. (The same as Maltby, in Yorkshire)
SCRATBY   Scrauti's village. (Another nickname; a 'person given to display')

Suffolk
BARNBY   Biarni's village. (The same as Barmby and Barnaby)

Westmorland
COLBY   Koli's village. (Common personal name)
NATEBY   Perhaps from a Norse personal name Nate, but perhaps from 'nettle', used either as a nickname or as the plant name)
SOULBY   Sule's village. (There is another Soulby, in Cumberland)

Durham
AISLABY   Alsakr's village. (There is another Aislaby in Yorkshire)

The Coming of the Vikings

Derbyshire
STAINSBY   Steinn's village

Cheshire
FRANKBY   Frakki's village

Warwickshire
RUGBY   Hroca's village. (The furthest west of the Midland 'bys')

Generally we must suppose that the personal name in the name of a village would be that of the leader of the settlement. Sometimes, however, a village was named from a group of people who followed the same calling. Flotmanby in Yorkshire means 'The sailors' village'; Hunmanby, also in Yorkshire, was 'the dog-keepers' village'; and Sutterby, in Lincolnshire, was 'the shoe-makers' village'.

A few settlements have as their first element an indication of the nationality of the group of people who lived there. They were generally Scandinavian villages isolated by the English villages which surrounded them. Thus, Danby, in the North Riding of Yorkshire, means 'The Danes' village. Denaby, in the West Riding, and Denby in Derbyshire have the same meaning. To be given these names, Scandinavian settlement cannot have been usual in the immediate area. In Normanby, Normanton, and Normacot (Staffs) Norwegians are particularized, and so are Frisians in Firsby and Ferrensby. The curious combination of elements in Ingleby in Derbyshire—the village of the English—must mean a remaining but isolated English settlement in an otherwise purely Scandinavian district.

Two other Scandinavian elements whose meaning is settlement are 'thorpe' and 'toft'. They are not so numerous as the 'bys' but they are widespread. A thorpe, as we have said, is a sign of Danish occupation rather than Norwegian and the original meaning was 'newly reclaimed land'. The probability is that a thorpe was a dependent farm belonging to a village. Thorpes often have a first element indicating their geographical relationship to another place, probably a larger village. Examples are Astrop (east thorpe) in Northamptonshire, Westrip (west thorpe) in Gloucester, and Southrop, also in Gloucester. Thorpes were far less important than bys and was often simply called 'The Thorpe'. Later a distinguishing element was added. In the *Oxford Dic-*

The Coming of the Vikings

tionary of English Place-names two columns of close print are given to composite 'thorpe' place-names. Mablethorpe in Lincolnshire and Thorpe Arch in Yorkshire are examples. Mablethorpe is Malbert's Thorpe. Malbert is an Old French personal name of Old German origin. 'Thwaite' is another Scandinavian element with much the same meaning as thorpe but it was also used for meadowland. It is to be found where Norsemen settled, i.e. in the north-west and extreme north. The thwaites in the Lake District are ubiquitous; Tilberthwaite is an instance. It means 'Tilli's clearing'. Seathwaite is another; it means 'The clearing on the lake' (Seathwaite Tarn).

The Scandinavian element 'toft' originally meant the site of a house and its outbuildings. From this sense developed such meanings as 'near a house' or 'homestead'. The expression 'toft and croft'—a dwelling and small-holding—has been in common use for many centuries and still figures in legal documents. The place-name 'toft' is mainly found in the East Midlands and in Yorkshire though there is Toft in Cheshire. Examples are Toft in Cambridgeshire, Lowestoft in Suffolk, meaning Hlothver's toft and Toft Monks in Norfolk. This last was, in the Middle Ages, a village belonging to the Abbey of Preaux in Normandy.

So much for the distribution of Scandinavian settlement and place-names which, it is clear, were much influenced by the treaty made between Alfred and Guthrum. This treaty lasted for Alfred's lifetime. He died in the year 900. His son, Edward, succeeded him. Edward re-conquered the Danelaw and incorporated the Danish territory with Wessex and Eastern Mercia to form what was the first truly English kingdom. He was greatly aided by his sister Ethelfleda, known as the Lady of Mercia. Edward was a wise and strong ruler and a master of military strategy. Ethelfleda had been married, at the age of fourteen, to the Earl of Mercia, a province which had been sadly ravaged by Scandinavian raids. The Earl who, it is thought, may have been an invalid, could do little to defend it. While Ethelfleda was still quite young, she took over the responsibility of government and, on her husband's death, became the ruler of Mercia under her brother, King Edward. Ethelfleda is an intriguing figure. She is said to have adopted a man's garments, grown a beard and fought side by side with the soldiers of Edward's army. Certainly she must have had great physical strength and endurance for her recorded journeys during the war against the Danes are astonish-

The Coming of the Vikings

ing in their length and frequency. The following is an extract from the *Anglo-Saxon Chronicle*:

In this year (913) by the grace of God, Ethelfleda, the Lady of the Mercians, went with all the Mercians to Tamworth and built the fortress there early in the summer and afterwards that at Stafford before Lammas (August).
Then in this, the following year, was fortified that fortress at Eddisbury (Cheshire) in early summer; and later in the same year . . . that at Warwick.

The building of these and other fortresses was part of the military tactics in conquering the Danelaw. Because of the increase in fortified places and the uses to which they were put, there was a proliferation of the place-name 'borough' and new meanings were attached to the term. 'Borough' is derived from the Anglo-Saxon word 'burgh' meaning a fortified place. In Anglo-Saxon times the term was applied to pre-historic, iron-age or Roman forts; Cadbury and Roxborough are examples. We have seen the importance of the stockaded camps made by the Danes in their invasions of this country. These strongholds were also called 'burghs' by the English. Some of Alfred's successes against the Danes were the result of his having built similar defended places. Edward and Ethelfleda developed and improved this feature of military strategy, sometimes using the remains of old Roman forts but also creating new ones.

The burghs or boroughs built by Edward and Ethelfleda consisted of camps on elevated ground, surrounded by a rough stone wall, topped by a wooden pallisade and protected by multiple earth-works. When old Roman forts were used the available stones in the ruins were used to repair the walls. These burghs were established at intervals in a great arc running from Chester, through Manchester, Bakewell, Derby, Stafford to Warwick. Many of them can still be seen. The best preserved, because it has not been built over or greatly disturbed, is at Eddisbury, between Northwich and Chester. The site is about an acre in extent. The inner ditch is well defined and clearly visible, and there are traces of two others. The place-name Eddisbury means Edward's burgh or borough. Eddisbury was one of a chain of forts which included Chester, Eddisbury, Runcorn, Warburton and Manchester. This group was well placed to contain the Norsemen in the Wirral at Kirby, Frankby, Raby and other places and they also served to prevent further invasion inland. All burghs were garrisoned.

The Coming of the Vikings

To provide maintenance for the garrisons and to keep the burghs in repair, the old Anglo-Saxon units of local government, the hundreds, were grouped into shires. The households of the shires were required to furnish men, money, food and labour. This is the origin of the English county. The principal burgh in each shire became the seat of administration and was, later, called the county town. A shire reeve or sheriff was appointed by the king. Because the principal burghs came to be associated with a unit of local government, the word 'borough' came to be associated with it too. County towns and other considerable settlements with some degree of local government also came to be known as boroughs, even though the term was not embodied in the place-name. Boroughs were places of relative safety. The machinery of government, though primitive, was present to restrain theft, fraud and violence. The practice grew of offering goods for sale in the shelter of their fortifications and this attracted increasing numbers of buyers and sellers. Boroughs thus often became market towns. The place-name Market Harborough in Leicestershire sums up this process very neatly.

The Danes of the Danelaw also fortified their larger settlements. The most important of these were Derby, Nottingham, Stamford, Leicester and Lincoln. They were known as the 'five boroughs'. Edward and Ethelfleda conquered each one in turn and incorporated them into the English system of government. All of them except Stamford became county towns, and Stamford on the London-Edinburgh road became an important market. Derby gave its name to the new county—Derbyshire—which is the only English county with a place-name containing a Scandinavian element. The only instance of feminine feeling recorded of Ethelfleda was connected with the storming of Derby. The gates of the town were breached and, in the fierce fighting that followed, 'four of her thanes, who were dear to her, were slain there within the gates'. She wept bitterly.

The building of burghs was not confined to the military under the king's authority. During the troubled centuries of the Scandinavian invasions many houses and farms were fortified; or villages would provide themselves with a refuge against marauding Danes and Norsemen. There are many place-names that contain the element 'burgh', and while not all belong to this cause or period, many do. It is not always possible to distinguish the older burghs from those associated with the Scandinavian invasions. The surest way is by expert examination of the site or excavation. Some place-names, however, give reliable clues in that Danish or Norse elements are included with burghs. Scarborough, on the Yorkshire coast, is a case in point. According to the Old Norse Kormak's saga, Skareaborg was built by Thorgils Skaroi, the date being about 965. Scarborough thus means Skaroi's burgh. Skaroi is a nickname meaning 'hare-lip'. Burton Stather is another indication—the fortified ton. Stather is Norse for a landing place. Burton Thorpe speaks for itself.

Of the numerous Burys, Bursteads, and Burtons, something can often be deduced from their geographical situation. If they are in the Danelaw or other districts of Scandinavian settlement, they may have been forts erected by or against the invaders. If they are in the south of England, it is probable (though not certain) that they date from an earlier period. An Anglo-Saxon personal name attached to the '-burgh' element is surely a clue: Didsbury is Dyddi's burgh, and Dyddi was an Anglo-Saxon name, not a Danish. The two Didsburys, one in Lancashire and one in Cheshire, are likely to have been English fortifications against the Norsemen. It is probable that so too is Prestbury (the priest's bury) in Cheshire.

We have said that the invasion period was followed by a considerable mixture of populations, and the hybrid names touched on earlier are clear evidence of it. Further hybrids are:

Leicestershire
SLAWSTON   Slag's tun. (Norse plus Old English)
THRUSSINGTON   Thorstein's tun. (The same)
THRISLINGTON   Another Thorstein's tun

Norfolk
ASLACTON   Aslac's tun. (Norse plus Old English)
HELHOUGHTON   Helgi's tun. (The same)

Northamptonshire
STRIXTON   Strikr's tun

Nottinghamshire
OSBERTON   Osbeorn's tun. (Osbeorn is an Anglicized form of the Norse *Asbiorn*)
THRUMPTON   Thormund's tun

The Coming of the Vikings

Suffolk
FLOWTON   Floki's tun. (Norse plus Old English)
(There is also a Flowthorpe)
KETTLEBASTON   Ketilbiorn's tun. (Norse plus Old English. Variations of the element Ketil in a personal name are common: Kettering, Kettleburgh, Kedleston, Ketsby, etc.)

Yorkshire
BARMSTON   Beorn or Beormund's tun. (From a common Scandinavian personal name found also in Barmpton, Barmby, Barmborough)
SCRUTON   Scrufa's tun. A hybrid including a Norse nickname for someone who is literally scurvy. A Danish leader of this name is mentioned in the *Anglo-Saxon Chronicle*
BROTHERTON   Probably from Norse personal names Broder or Brodor. They mean 'brother'
THURSTON   Thurulf's tun. This Norse personal name has many variants; it occurs wherever the Norsemen settled

After the conflicts of the English and Danes, and after the settlement and the assimilation of the two populations to each other, England gradually emerged in the tenth century as a unified kingdom again. The last Danish king was killed in battle in 921; and, though there was yet another century of trouble, the Danes were nothing like as difficult to deal with as in earlier days. They had now given hostages to fortune: they now possessed villages and towns which could be plundered in return, if they raided English settlements.

In the early eleventh century there was a brief interlude of foreign Danish rule, when under Canute and his sons England was incorporated into a short-lived Scandinavian empire. On the death of the last of Canute's sons independence returned under Edward the Confessor.

Canute's invasion and reign can be dealt with shortly, for it had little effect upon place-names. Only a handful seem to have been created at this period. South of London where there is little other evidence of Scandinavian settlements there are two villages whose names contain Danish elements: Swainston, in the Isle of Wight, and Thurloxton, in Somerset. It will be seen that these are both hybrids. There is also an East Garston, in Berkshire. It is thought that these places and a few others might have been estates given to Canute's followers—perhaps to members of his bodyguard.

Several settlements have names which embody the name Canute itself, and the question always arises of whether they refer to *the* Canute. There is Knuston, in Northamptonshire, and Knotton, in Staffordshire, and Knutsford, in Cheshire. Canute was a fairly common Danish personal name, and most cases of such place-names probably have no connection with the king. Knutsford is the most likely to have had such a connection. The town itself boldly proclaims it, but much more important than this is the documentary evidence for Canute's presence for a short time in Manchester, which is only twelve miles distant. The ford the name refers to may perhaps have been constructed by the king for the passage of his army as he travelled north from East Anglia. Near the centre of Manchester there is a district called Knott Mill, and this has inevitably led to a claim that the king established a mill there. This is pure speculation.

Field-names are not in the scope of this book, but it is worth mentioning that the evidence they offer shows that there was a wide distribution of Scandinavian elements in districts where the place-names are Anglo-Saxon. For instance, in parts of east Lancashire, and in the Dane Valley, which forms part of the boundary between Cheshire and Staffordshire. Investigations at this level might well fill in more details of the Scandinavian settlement.

Chapter 7
The Normans and After

It seems that 1066 is the date that everybody remembers. In that year William of Normandy, with a few thousand knights and their followers, defeated the English army at the battle of Hastings and was afterwards crowned King of England. In the course of the next few years the English estates were parcelled out among the Norman knights and new baronies were created for the more important adventurers as a reward for their support of William in his now successful venture. There was a pro-Norman party among the English, especially in the south of the country, and many of these were left in possession of their land though sometimes with a Norman overlord. In the North, two years after the Conquest, there was a rebellion which was defeated with great destruction and bloodshed. William is reported to have sworn to leave not a man or a horse nor even a goose alive between Tyne and Humber, and although this terrible threat was not absolutely fulfilled, several generations passed before the North recovered from the devastation which accompanied William's campaign of suppression. Normans were given estates left ownerless by death or confiscation and very few English landholders remained.

The Norman Conquest was an event of the utmost importance for the life and civilization of this country, and in the end every aspect of English social life was deeply changed as a result of it. It is no longer possible to take up a simple attitude, either for or against the Conquest. In some respects its results were, in the long term, beneficial. In others they were disastrous. The civilization they conquered, and in the end overthrew, was by the time the Normans came no longer the simple, vigorous and practical thing it had been in the early days. (The period between the coming of the English and the coming of the Normans—the whole span, that is, of Anglo-Saxon England—lasted six hundred years; about as long, that is, as the time that has elapsed between the Black

The Normans and After

Death and the present. This period too easily gets telescoped in the mind, and thought of as much more uniform than it really was.) If we compare the civilization of England on the eve of the Norman invasion with the civilization of the Normans themselves, there is no doubt which was the more developed, complex and sophisticated. In art, literature, scholarship and even in architecture, the work of the English was much in advance. A great deal was lost in the aftermath of the Conquest, which was never replaced. On the other hand the English kingdom was unruly and unstable, 'relying for existence on a military system which recent events had shown to be insufficient for its needs'. These words are those of Sir Frank Stenton, written towards the end of his great book, *Anglo-Saxon England*. His opinion of the Conquest, with which he closes his book, was:

The Normans who entered into the English inheritance were a harsh and violent race. They were closest of all western peoples to the barbarian strain in the continental order. They had produced little in art or learning, and nothing in literature, that could be set beside the work of Englishmen. But politically, they were the masters of their world.

The gift which, above all, they brought to their new kingdom was the gift that allowed them to win it: a genius for government and war.

The compilation of *Domesday Book* is the most striking single example of the administrative imagination and drive of the Conqueror. Since it is also the most valuable single document for the student of English place-names, it is justifiable to dwell on it a little.

There have been many opinions amongst historians as to William's motives in having this great survey drawn up—a survey which was planned to list all the manors in the kingdom, with their value in plough-teams and stock, and also in men—serfs and freemen, farmers and cottagers. The king wanted to know what he owned, and what his subjects owned. The detail he required was unusual for its age, and was disturbing to contemporaries. The account of the decision to make the survey is given in the *Anglo-Saxon Chronicle* (which, in spite of its name, was continued into the Norman period; the last entry, in the last of its various manuscripts, was made well into the twelfth century). The chronicler apparently finds something shocking in the earthy details that were to be asked for:

So very narrowly he caused it to be searched out that there was not a single hide nor a yard of land nor even—it is shame to tell though it seemed to him no shame to do—an ox, nor a cow, nor a swine was left that was not set down...

The decision was taken during a council held by William at Gloucester in 1085, at Christmas-time. This was getting towards twenty years since the battle of Hastings, and it is interesting to notice that the information was to relate not only to the present state of the realm, but also to the state in which it was on the day on which King Edward 'was alive and dead'—the day, that is, from which William claimed to have inherited the throne. (The reign of Harold was of course an illegitimate usurpation from William's point of view.)

The method of making the survey was that of holding inquests up and down the land, presided over by royal commissioners who had themselves no interests in the areas in which they worked. At the inquests, sworn juries testified to the information wanted, and their evidence was taken down. It ultimately, probably after a second checking by another group of commissioners, found its way to the court. The final compilation of the single two-volume *Domesday Book* followed the completion of the survey.

It would be a mistake to expect that the survey would have been carried out with the completeness of, shall we say, the ten-yearly census of the present day. Even within the brief they were given, there were gaps left by the commissioners; and some items of information which a modern ruler would wish for—an exact count of the actual population, rather than of the heads of households, for instance—were not sought. Some districts especially in the north were omitted from the survey, and even within the districts which were covered in detail there are gaps. Towns are not consistently surveyed, and both London and Winchester are omitted. These shortcomings appear perhaps unduly large to modern scholars, tantalized by the lack of fine details which, for any other eleventh-century kingdom, it would be unreasonable to expect. The survey matched the achievements of the Roman Empire itself, in the field of administration.

Its importance for the study of place-names is easily shown. To take a random example, the first two hundred main entries in Ekwall's dictionary, under the letter C, can be divided according to whether the name first appears in the *Domesday Book*, whether it appears before, or whether it appears after. The results are:

        Before *Domesday Book*   32
        In *Domesday Book*   85
        After *Domesday Book*   83

If every aspect of the social life of this country was deeply affected by the Conquest, the results on the English language must accordingly have been both profound and extensive. This, too, affects the history of place-names.

The Conqueror and his companions, although descended from the same Norsemen who had done such damage in earlier centuries, were speakers of French, and as a result of the Conquest there were again two languages in use in England.

Norman-French became the language of the court and of the landholders and aristocracy, but English remained the language of the bulk of the population. In this sort of situation, which has arisen before in other places, something curious tends to happen. The language of the conquered takes into itself very many words out of the conquerors' language, but the converse does not happen. Words flow downwards, that is to say, not upwards between the classes. English became a language which, whilst remaining fully a Germanic tongue, had a very large foreign element in its vocabulary. Later, when the Norman court and nobility of England had lost its close links with France, Norman-French died out in England, and English became again the language of government, law, and culture in general; but it was now English of a rather different nature. The vocabulary had been enlarged, but other things had happened to it too. One thing, which may be mentioned here for completeness, was that a process of alteration to the basic grammar of English had been hastened by the Conquest and its aftermath. The process had begun before the Normans arrived, and the exact details of the effect of the Conquest on it would take us too far from our present theme: but an effect there certainly was. A second development closely linked with this one was the acceleration of the formation of divergent local dialects within English. The language ceased to be the means of government and country-wide communication; it ceased to be, what it had earlier been, a language of education

The Normans and After

and of literature; and as a result the centrifugal tendencies which are always alive in a language were given free play by the withdrawal of these conservative influences. English developed a rich pattern of local dialects in consequence. These have had a considerable influence upon our place-names. Not upon the establishment of the place-names, but upon their transmission through the centuries. We shall return to the question of the relations of dialect and place-names at a later point.

To understand the effect of the Conquest upon English place-names it is important to be clear about the differences between this invasion, and that one six centuries before which had brought the English to England. The earlier one had been a migration of peoples, moving as tribes under their leaders to establish themselves on the new lands. The Great Trek of the Boers would be a more recent parallel; and so would the westward movement of the North American frontier during the eighteenth and nineteenth centuries. In the fifth century the previous population—the Celts—were mostly either assimilated, destroyed or displaced. From this point there began the great place-name-giving period of our history. This was an invasion of settlers. In contrast, the Norman Conquest was much less an invasion than a take-over operation. It is likely that the total number of people who actually moved into England was fairly small: some say about 20,000 in all; of which 6,000 fought at Hastings. They left the English on the ground where their ancestors had established themselves—all but those who suffered by war, or the dreadful devastation of the North. The Normans merely imposed a foreign aristocracy upon the native population, replacing the earls and ealdormen whom they had formerly served. Just as the English language remained the speech of the ordinary men and women, so their old place-names remained in use. It is clear that comparatively few new Norman place-names came into use as a consequence of the events of 1066; though they were, of course, not absent entirely.

The first, and probably the most important effect upon place-names of the new Norman rule was the creation of names such as Ashby-de-la-Zouch, Dunham Massey or Holme Lacy: names which have a Norman personal name added to the original English name. Dunham Massey, in Cheshire, was originally simply Dunham: the ham on the hill. Harvo de Masei was a Norman knight who had supported William at the battle of

The Normans and After

Hastings. He was made a baron, under Hugh Lupus, the newly created Earl of Chester. Harvo de Masei built a fortified manor house at Dunham and ruled his barony from there. The place is called Dunham in the Domesday record; by the twelfth century it was known as 'Dunham Massy'. The *e* was added later. Another example is Holme Lacy in Herefordshire. Roger de Laci, a French knight, was given the place in reward of his support of William. Ashby-de-la-Zouch takes the latter part of its place-name from a French family name, 'Souch'.

Dorset and Somerset are rich in double place-names. Not all of them stem back to the Conquest, though some of them do; Oakford Fitzpaine and Hardington Mandeville are examples Hardington was an early Anglo-Saxon settlement; the place-name means 'the village of Heardred's people'. It was granted to Galfridus de Mondville who came from a town of that name in Normandy. Shepton Mallet and Shepton Beauchamp were originally named as sheep farms. Both came into the hands of French or Norman knights whose names were then added to the place-name.

The castles which the Normans built, for protection in the first place against possible English risings, later for protection against each other, are still very conspicuous features of the country-side. Many places have *castle* itself as part of their names, and this is a French word which came into English in this period. Because of this, however, it should not be assumed that such places are always sites where Norman castles were built. Once the word was in the language, it was applied also to fortifications of much earlier date. Maiden Castle is a case in point: this is an Iron Age fortress. It could also be applied to fortifications of a much later date, or to houses whose fortifications were merely ornamental, or to houses without fortifications at all. Castle Howard in Yorkshire is one such. This magnificent mansion was built in the very early eighteenth century by Sir John Vanbrugh, for the Howard family. It was built at a place which was formerly called Hinderskelfe, but which is now called by the name of the house.

There is a further point which again reduces the likelihood that a place with castle in its name commemorates a true Norman castle: that is, the process of popular etymology, a number of names may have been altered to look as if 'Castle' was originally part of them, though being in the beginning quite different. Castleford, in West Yorkshire, was originally *Ceaster-ford*—'the

The Normans and After

ford by the Roman fort'. (The first occurrence of the name comes at the year 948 in the *Anglo-Saxon Chronicle*.) Castlett in Glamorganshire is 'the valley of the wild cats'. Finally, we should remember that there was a British word castello, which is found in Castle Carrock in Cumberland, and in such places as Castlemaugham in Cornwall, which, whilst referring to a fort, have no Norman-French connection at all. (The Celtic word came from a borrowing of the Latin *castellum* at a period much earlier than the Conquest.)

When all this is said, however, it remains true that most names with the word *castle* in them refer to Norman castles, whether or not these have survived on the ground up to the present. At first these were wooden structures, placed upon a mound and protected by ditches. Later, many of these were replaced by stone strongholds surrounded by an elaborate system of moats and walls. The memory and, indeed, the ruins of these castles are to be found at Castle Acre and Castle Rising in Norfolk and at Castleton in Derbyshire. Sometimes a French or Norman descriptive name was given to the castle. The name generally refers to the scenery with which the castle was surrounded. The following all contain the adjective 'beau'—beautiful:

BEAMISH	Durham. The beautiful mansion
BEAUFRONT	Northumberland. The beautiful brow
BEAUMANOR	Leicestershire. The beautiful manor
BEAULIEU	Hampshire. The beautiful place
BEAUVALE	Nottinghamshire. The beautiful vale
BEAUMARIS	Anglesey. The beautiful sea. A castle built by Edward I after the conquest of Wales.

A variation is Belvoir, in Leicestershire, the beautiful view.

The Normans were also great builders of churches. The name of the saint to whom the church was dedicated was sometimes added to the name of the village. It is not possible to be sure from the dedication place-name that the original church was a Norman foundation—the Norman structure may have replaced a Saxon church, for Saxon churches were often built of wood, not stone. Nevertheless, a dedication place-name is sometimes a pointer to the Norman period. There is a cluster of this type of place-name inland from the Wash—Sutton St James, Walpole St Andrew and Walpole St Peter, Terrington St Clement and Terrington St John, and many others. Dorset and Somerset also have similar

The Normans and After

place-names—Sydling St Andrew and Ottery St Mary are examples. There are other dedication place-names which possibly date from the Norman period scattered about the country—St Nicholas at Wade in Kent and St Michael on Wyre, in Lancashire, are probabilities.

In the period between the eleventh and fourteenth centuries, many monasteries were built in England. The majority were daughter foundations from French monastic houses and often the English foundations were given French or Frenchified names. This name often became a place-name for the settlement in the environs. Rievaulx in Yorkshire is a French translation of Ryedale, the original name which still survives for the valley in which Rievaulx is set. (It is itself a hybrid form: a British river-name with an English word *dale* added.) Rievaulx was a large and important monastery, founded by the Cistercian order in the twelfth century. Dieulacres, near Leek in Staffordshire, is another example. The Earls of Chester had a hunting lodge in the forest of Leek; the fourth Earl, Randle II, died in this lodge suddenly after a heavy day's hunting. The story goes that his son, Randle Blundeville, also Earl of Chester, had a dream while sleeping at the lodge in which his father appeared to him and enjoined Randle to build a monastery at that place 'for the repose of his father's soul'. Blundeville awakened his wife and told her of his father's request, to which she replied, 'Dieu la cres', which can be roughly translated, 'God speed it'. The story is perhaps true: but the name itself is of a type which is found also in Gracedieu, in Leicestershire ('God's Grace'), and Haltemprice, in East Yorkshire ('High Enterprise')—a type which we may call the 'Motto' type.[1] The name Dieulacres is remembered now only by local antiquaries, but the other two names survive. So too does Fountains, in Yorkshire—an abbey which takes its name from the presence of springs. Blanchland, in Northumberland—in the twelfth century, Blanchelande—means 'White Glade'. Grosmont —in French, 'big hill'—was a daughter monastery established in North Yorkshire from the mother priory at Grosmont in France.

The addition of French personal names to English place-names; then names of castles, churches and monasteries—these are the main groups of French place-names we can distinguish, and they do not add up to a great many. For the rest, there are no obvious subdivisions into which we can sort Norman-French

[1] These are both also the names of monasteries.

The Normans and After

names. A glance down the following list, however, which is merely a random selection of some of the more interesting other names with French origins or association, will perhaps show up one general point fairly clearly: few of these fall into the category of primary habitation-names. They refer to hills, woods, moors, and boundaries: places where secondary settlements were founded as the population increased.

MALPAS	Cheshire. From *Malo passu*, the difficult passage. There is another Malpas in Cornwall
BATTLE	Sussex. Named after the battle of Hastings
BOULGE	Suffolk. From French *bouge*, meaning 'uncultivated ground covered with heather or rough grass'
COWDRAY PARK	Sussex. From French *coudraie*, a hazel copse
DEVIZES	Wiltshire. From French *devises*, a boundary. (No one knows which boundary!)
CHAPEL EN LE FRITH	Derbyshire. The chapel in the forest. A chapel was built here in the thirteenth century by Richard Peveril. (*Frith* is an English word)
HAUTBOIS	Norfolk. From the French *haut bois*, high wood
RIDGMONT	Bedfordshire and East Riding of Yorkshire. The red hill. From Rougemont in France. Popular etymology has made this name more like *ridge*
MOUNTSORREL	Leicester. Sorrel-coloured hill. The place had a strong Norman castle
EGREMONT	Cumberland. From the French *aigremont*, a sharp, pointed hill
KEARSNEY	Kent. From French *cressoinere*, place where cresses grow
STOKESEY	Shropshire. This was originally the English name 'Stoke': and the ending *sei* is a family name. One Hugh de Sei held the manor in twelfth century. The name is therefore of the same form as Seaton Delaval, Holme Lacy, etc.

The Normans and After

If French did not contribute many to the total of English place-names, its influence was important in other ways, for instance, in the spelling and pronunciation of many names.

The scribes who wrote up the records which went to the making of *Domesday Book*, and their many successors in the following centuries, were often French. There were sounds in French which did not occur in English; and English had sounds which did not occur in French. It also had combinations of sounds which, whilst existing separately in French, did not occur together. People in general, once they have passed the stage of childhood, are very resistant to new sounds they may be required to put their tongues to: they frequently substitute sounds from their own language, if such exist. Sometimes, as in the case of 'h' sounds, they may omit them altogether. Frenchmen today, until they have learned English sufficiently well, will drop their 'aitches'. The Norman scribe would be no more skilful at the sound.

In the centuries after the *Domesday Book*, the spelling conventions of French were devised to fit that language, not English: and they would be the only conventions the scribe knew. They would have difficulties in applying them to the new sounds they heard. Often, a sound that occurred in English would have a spelling in French different from the conventional English one. It would be natural for the scribe to get the name down in a French spelling.

Sometimes we come across an inverted spelling. The example of Abney will illustrate what this means. 'Abney' means Abba's island. It never had an initial 'h'-sound. When the Chronicle scribe spells it, therefore, Habenai, he is probably not intending to suggest that an 'h'-sound is to be heard. He knows that the spelling of many French words starts with an 'h'-sound, which was no longer pronounced, and perhaps assumes it would be more 'correct' to spell the English name Abney with a similar unpronounced 'h'.

P. H. Reaney, in *The Origin of English Place-Names*, gives a detailed account of the name Scrobbesbyrigseir—a name that presented problems to record-keepers even before the Conquest. The first two parts of this three-part name present a familiar pattern: a personal name (in the possessive) followed by one of the more common place-name elements; in this case, *byrig*, which is a form of the word 'burh', meaning fortress. Since *sc* in Old

The Normans and After

English is pronounced *sh*, it is perhaps clear that the last part of the form is the word 'shire'. The first part is the name of one Scrob—a man for whose existence there is independent evidence. The name means 'the shire of Scrob's fortress'. This is the shape the name had in the *Anglo-Saxon Chronicle* at the year 1006. ('Then the king went over the Thames into Scrobbesbyrigscir, and there received the entertainment due to him, at the time of midwinter.') Shortly afterwards, however, the middle element dropped out of the records, and there was left Scropscire: a form which could, and did, lead fairly easily to the modern pronunciation 'Shropshire'. But, somewhat later than this, in *Domesday Book*, an extra vowel has come into the word, between the 'sr' and the 'r'; for the French even then were not happy with some consonant combinations. They wrote, Sciropescir. After this, the initial 'sh'-sound became 's'; and the 'r', by a process which is on the surface unconvincing but in fact is linguistically quite respectable, was changed to an 'l' sound. (When the comic-paper writer makes his Chinese substitute 'l's for 'r's, he is testifying to the connection between the two sounds.) In this way, there arrived the form Silopshire; and also Salopshire. The modern form 'Salop' comes about in this way. Today people have even started using it in speech, as well as in writing.

The combination of 's' and 'n' at the beginning of a word was another difficulty for the Norman-French. (There is something strange about this combination in English, for most words that start with it have derogatory or unpleasant meanings: sneer; sneak; snob; snide, etc.) They tended to let the 's' drop out, and so Snotingaham, as it was in 922, has given us the modern Nottingham. The county name was altered in the same way; Snotingehamscyre in *Domesday Book*. (Snotingaham means the settlement of the followers of Snot. The name Snot had the meaning 'wise'.) In a similar way the Lancashire name Trafford lost an initial 's'. This place is very close to Stretford, in the outer environs of Manchester, and its own name was still Stratford in one record dated 1206, whilst in another of about the same time the change has already taken place.

Some words which should have begun with a 'Y' had the spelling 'J' given to them, since initial 'Y' was unknown to the Normans, and this in time affected the pronunciation. (Incidentally, 'J' is among the rarest of all letters to start English place-names. Ekwall gives less than a dozen in all. Only 'X' (with none)

The Normans and After

and 'Z' (with four) have fewer entries in his dictionary.) Jarrow, Jervaulx, Jevington and Jesmond would have started with 'y'-sounds if there had been no Conquest. Jervaux is a form of 'Uredale'; Jevington is 'the tun of Geofa's folk'; and Jesmond is the mouth of the Ouse—Gese-muthe in 1275. 'Mond' has been substituted for 'mouth' in this very Frenchified name.

The name of 'Cirencester' has always attracted attention, and occasional flutters of letters to *The Times* about its proper pronunciation. Some of its natives pronounce it 'sissiter', others pronounce it 'syren-sester', and most strangers find some variant between these two. The last element of this name is the one which occurs elsewhere as either '-chester', or (in the Scandinavian areas) '-caster'. The French baulked at the 'tch' pronunciation, then as they do today. They substituted for it the simple *s* sound, pronouncing this ending 'sester'. This pronunciation eventually conquered the traditional one. (The spelling with a *c* shows that at this period, speakers of French gave this letter the value it has in such words as cease, peace, etc.) All the other places which are spelt '-cester' can be explained in the same way: Towcester, Gloucester, Worcester, etc.

This accounts for the ending of Cirencester. As for the beginning, precisely the same thing happened. *Ciren* is the Frenchman's attempt to pronounce the name 'Churn'—again with the awkward 'tch' sound in it. This word is the name of a Celtic tribe (mentioned incidentally by Ptolemy who wrote in the second century). It is also the name of the river on which the town stands—a name which it may have acquired from the name of the town in its Old English form, or independently from the name of the tribe.

Finally, some miscellaneous examples. Durham is a Norman attempt to pronounce Dunholm, 'island with a hill'. (Dunholm is the form the name has in the *Anglo-Saxon Chronicle*.)

Knighton—a frequent name, meaning 'the tun of the knights' —that is, the personal retainers of a lord—appears in five entries in the *Domesday Book* with the spelling Chenistetone. This is the result of an attempt to represent by French conventions the English sound of Knighton, in which the *k* and the *gh* parts would be separately pronounced.

Chapter 8
Curiosities

In earlier chapters we have looked at the fortunes of the peoples who have lived in this country, as seen in the light that may be shed by place-names. This chapter reverses this procedure, and in it we consider the fortunes which place-names encounter as a result of their use by people.

Anyone who looks any distance into the history of place-names is struck by the fact of change. A few names, a very few, still preserve the forms in which they made their first entry into history; but usually we must see the present form as the result of a long story of development. Ewshott, in Hampshire—'the yew grove'—appears first as Iweschate; Hanworth in Norfolk is found in the *Domesday Book* as Haganaworda. Some of the changes are changes in spelling conventions; others represent actual changes in the pronunciation of the names. These last, in detail, are primarily matters for the historical linguist. There are however some types of change worth looking at fairly closely before passing them over to the experts, since they offer interesting sidelights on the history of our language.

One such process is that known as popular etymology. Etymology itself, which is the business of making clear the origins and history of a word, is a complex undertaking that requires great patience and expertise. Popular etymology is a smaller thing, but one which produces more obvious results. It means those changes made in the form of a word by a mistaken feeling by its users about what it supposedly derives from. An example or two from common nouns rather than from place-names will illustrate what this means. There was a word in French which referred to a sort of marine creature; the word 'crevice'. This was borrowed into English during the fifteenth century, and was then mistakenly thought to have as its last syllable the word *fish*. By the sixteenth century this had caused it to become *crayfish*, and it has remained so ever since. True etymology shows that the

Curiosities

word had in origin nothing to do with fish; popular etymology assumes that it has, and adapts the word to make the connection clearer. True etymology belongs in the study and the library; popular etymology works first in the street and in the market place; and ultimately, in the study and the library as well. In a similar way, some dialect speakers describe their ailments as 'screwmatics'. 'If that isn't what "rheumatics" really means,' one can hear them saying, 'then it ought to mean it, for it feels like it.' They may call the asparagus by the homelier name 'sparrow-grass'; and use the name 'gillyflower' for the plant which originally had the French name *giroflé*. This has as little of the flower in it as 'crayfish' has of fish. The process is found at all periods, in almost all languages. It is one which no one could stop, even if one wanted to try—and perhaps only a pedant would make the attempt. This process is important in place-name study because of the false trails it lays. It often seems that, once words have become place-names, they now follow courses different from those same words which remain in the language at large. They come to lose their appearance of identity with each other. This fact of linguistic history is offset by the persistent habit people have of trying to make as much sense as possible of the words they find available to use. Now and again, they make the wrong sort of sense of it; and the result is a name which does not mean what it so obviously seems to mean.

FIFIELD in Oxfordshire, near Stow-on-the-Wold, is not a clear name at first glance; *field* offers few problems, but the prefixed *fi-* is not a familiar one. The truth is that what seems most obvious here is in fact most misleading. In *Domesday Book*, the place figures as Fifhide; and the ending of this form is clearly not the word *field*, which would have been spelled *feld*, but the word *hide*—120 acres of arable land—the amount that could be cultivated with one ox-team. A man of five hides would therefore be someone of substance. This was the normal holding of a man of the rank of thane.

The same name—five hide—produces also the modern form Fifehead; there are two examples in Dorset.

ALICE HOLT FOREST in Hampshire is the sort of name around which legends spring up. One can imagine Alice as a young heroine to whom some misfortune occurred in the woods, and who was no doubt rescued by some Lochinvar figure. Or perhaps she was a witch? She was neither of these things, but a rather

Curiosities

desperate attempt of the local imagination to make some sort of acceptable sense of a name which occurs first in 1169 as Alfisholt, and which is, according to Ekwall, Aelfsige's holt or wood. The Forest attached to the modern form repeats the sense of Holt, and perhaps was added at a time when the meaning of Holt was getting forgotten. It is like the hybrid name Chetwode, in Berkshire, which adds wood to the end of a Celtic name which already means wood. 'Wood Wood.')

There was in Old English a word *bremel*, which meant *bramble*. It is indeed the same word; the 'b' sound has crept into it in the intervening centuries in the same way as it crept also into thimble; or as a 'k' sound is, in the speech of some people today, arising in a word like length ('lengkth'). Another place-name in which an extra consonant has crept into the middle is Bewdley, in Worcestershire. This is from the French *beau lieu*—'beautiful place'. Bremel is the basis of such names as Bramingham, Bramshott, and others. BREMHILL in Wiltshire is especially interesting, since, whilst it looks like 'the bramble hill', it is in fact no more than the word *bremel* itself, misinterpreted as *brem-hill*.

There is a BONEHILL in Staffordshire which is not a hill of bones, but probably a hill where bulls were to be found. In 1230 it appeared as Bolenhull; and the disappearance of the middle 'l' sound could have been hastened by the attempt to make it look more understandable. HOLYPORT has been altered, but whether this is a case of popular etymology based on a misunderstanding, a deliberate alteration made by people who understood the meaning only too well, as Ekwall thinks, is a matter of conjecture. In 1220 the form was Horipord, meaning a 'dirty market town'.

CLYST WILLIAM is a lovely name. It is partly taken from the river Clyst, which is one of those Celtic river-names which survived in so great numbers. William could be anyone; perhaps even a river god? No; he was born from a misunderstanding of Clistewelme, 'the source of the Clyst'. (The Old English word here is 'aewielm', spring.)

ROSE ASH, in Devon, might have been a girlhood friend of Alice Holt, or wooed by Clyst William; but instead she too is a fallacy. In *Domesday Book* the name is Aissa; later it is Esse (1242). Scholars have little hesitation in interpreting this as Ash tree. The prefixed Rose is recorded first in 1400, in the form Rowesassche—and is merely the possessive of the masculine name

Curiosities

Ralph. A Ralph de Ese was mentioned in this place in 1198, according to Ekwall.

Where a place-name contains fairly unusual elments, they are perhaps more likely to suffer this sort of change. In Gloucestershire there are the two Slaughters—LOWER SLAUGHTER and UPPER SLAUGHTER. These, together with the nearby SLAUGHTERFORD, incorporate a probable word 'slohtre', which was presumed to exist with the meaning of 'muddy place'. The change to the more picturesque and understandable present forms is understandable. The word occurs only in these three names. This explanation takes the romance out of the name, of course. If the reader is interested in names that preserve the record of bloody deeds, however, he can think of Morpeth—the murder path.

The suspicion that HALTWHISTLE in Northumberland has some reference to the operation of railways is one which many young minds must have entertained; and the knowledge that this is historically impossible leaves a puzzle. The explanation lies in the Old English word *twisla*, which means the fork of a river, or the junction of two streams. It occurs in Birtwisle, in Lancashire; Castweazel, in Kent; Oswaldtwistle, in Lancashire; and elsewhere. The first element in Haltwhistle is the French adjective *haut*, meaning 'high'. The name was Hautwisel in 1240.

SCHOLAR GREEN in Cheshire suggests some gentle academic pasture where philologists may safely browse; a name which would be perfectly appropriate if encountered somewhere in North Oxford. The first part of the name is a popular etymology of the Norse *skali*, a shed. This is found in the Scandinavian areas of England in more recognizable forms: Seascale, Laskill, Landskill, Summersgill, and, by itself, Scales, Scholes and Scole.

The next example is a case of mistaken etymology, not very appropriately called 'popular' as it is produced by minds of some degree of erudition. The only cathedral in Staffordshire is that of LICHFIELD; and this city has long religious associations. It was, at one time, the seat of a third Archbishop of the Church of England, though this did not last very long. The records of the name go back far into history: it occurs in the *Itinerary of Antonine* in the fourth century, in the form 'Letoceto'. This is a Latinized form of a Celtic place-name which alludes to a grey woodland (the parts of the name being akin to the Welsh *Llwyd*, meaning 'grey'; and *coed*, meaning 'wood'), and is the basis of the name Liccidfeld recorded in the eighth century by the Vener-

Curiosities

able Bede; the word 'field' added to it is not remarkable. (It did not mean what the modern word means—an area enclosed by walls or hedges. A field was an open tract of arable land. The use of it in the modern sense, replacing the word *close*, is fairly recent.) It happens, however, that there was an Old English word *lic*, pronounced 'leech', which meant corpse. This survives in dialect use; it is found in such old words as lykewake, a vigil kept over a dead body; and it is part of the word lychgate, the roofed entrance to a churchyard under which the bier may rest at a funeral. This is coincidence, and the name Lichfield has no connection with it; the place was called something like this, as we have seen, even before the Anglo-Saxons came to Britain. This has not prevented the growth of a legend around the name. To quote Isaac Taylor, a nineteenth-century scholar who wrote, in *Words and Places*, one of the early masterpieces of place-name study (but whose mastery did not prevent him being wrong):

At Lichfield in Staffordshire the city arms are a field surcharged with dead bodies. Tradition refers to the martyrdoms of a thousand Christian converts.

Taylor accepts these thousand martyrs, but there has never been any real evidence for them. The martyrs were invented to account for the name, which was mistakenly thought to mean 'field of the corpses', by people who had sufficient learning to know the meaning of 'lich' but too little historical understanding to avoid being misled by it.

The truth about Lichfield has been known for a very long time, but the myth still crops up. When, a few years ago, one of the writers of this book gently reproved a clergyman who had written a long letter in a local newspaper elaborating on the martyrs, and pointing out the facts of the matter, there was no real withdrawal; merely the reply that, even though there was perhaps no factual truth in the story, there was a great spiritual truth here, and in the light of this the real truth must take second place. The study of place-names has many incidental enjoyments to offer, as can be seen.

Back-formations

The process of back-formation resembles popular etymology to the extent of being the consequence of misunderstanding. What

Curiosities

happens here is that a word whose ending seems to be fairly regular—'er', for instance, or 'ing'—is taken to be made up out of a shorter word with that ending added to it, whereas in fact it is nothing of the sort. In language, mistakes repeated often enough cease to be mistakes. If from the word scissors sufficient people assumed the existence of a verb, *to sciss, then that verb would come to exist, and get into the dictionaries. The verb to beg came into being in just this way; the verb to buttle is now no more than half a joke, but the verb to swashbuckle is on its way to being fully established.

In the case of place-names, back-formation normally takes the form of assuming the existence of river-names, or personal-names, from the forms of other names which seem to contain them. The classic example is the name of the river CAM. This is the river upon which Cambridge is situated, and the visitor would naturally assume that the town obtained its name from it—'the bridge on the Cam'. This is a mistake. The traditional name of the river is the Granta. It occurs fairly well unchanged in the name of Grantchester. It is to be found in all the early forms of the name which is now Cambridge; Grantacaestir, in 730 (somewhat confusing, this one, because of the modern Grantchester); Grontabricc, ten or fifteen years later; and Grentebrige in *Domesday Book*. What happened in this case is that the 'Granta' form changed into the 'Cam' form, over a very long period. Grontabricc became Cambridge. (Part of the change was certainly due to Norman influence.) When this process was complete the next stage happened: the river Granta, which flowed through Cambridge but seems to have no connection with it in name, was renamed the Cam. This took place towards the end of the sixteenth century.

Other river-names came about in the same way. The river which flows through Arundel is now called the Arun, but was formerly called the Tarrant. Arundel means 'the valley where hoarhound grows'—from an Old English Harhun-dell. (As another example of popular etymology, 'hoarhound' the herb has no connection with the word 'hound', a dog.)

There are two rivers called the Rother, both formerly called something else. The Rother in West Sussex and Hampshire flows by Rotherbridge, a name which means 'The bridge for cattle'. The first part of this is the Old English word hryther, cattle. Misunderstood in fairly recent time as 'the bridge over the

Curiosities

Rother', this caused the river to be renamed and lose its earlier name of the Shire. The East Rother, in East Sussex and Kent, was formerly the Lympne. In this case it was Rotherfield which brought about the change.

Modern names

Etruria is a name for what was in ancient times a part of the peninsula of Italy, and it is also the name of a rather grim part of the city of Stoke-on-Trent, containing a station, a canal and a steelworks. Theories crop up from time to time which suggest that the ancient Etruscans visited Britain, and this name is sometimes cited as evidence. This is a mistake. The name Etruria dates only from the eighteenth century. It is the place where Josiah Wedgwood, the potter, established his factory, which remained there until the middle of the twentieth century, during which time the area had changed from being a village in the fields outside Burslem to what it now is. The name 'Etruria' arises from a misapprehension which Wedgwood shared with most of his contemporaries. In his day many ancient Greek vases were coming to light in Italy, which had been either exported there from the Greek homeland or produced there in the Greek colonies in southern Italy. For a while it was thought that these were the product of the Etruscan civilization, which was the one which flourished immediately before the rise of Rome to dominance; and during this time Wedgwood, who rightly admired these vases, named his own factory after their supposed home. The Etruscans did make pots of their own, but they were inferior to the Greek. There is elsewhere in the Potteries a place called Dresden, named after the more famous porcelain town in Germany.

These two examples remind us that the giving of new names to English places did not entirely end in the middle ages; Ekwall does not list modern names in his dictionary, being a purist in these matters, and other authorities are usually silent about them; but the traveller who encounters them may be no less curious about how they came into being.

A recent name will usually say what it means more clearly than an ancient one, for there will not have been time for the name to develop far from the rest of the language. Goodall's Corner, near Nantwich in Cheshire, requires no explanation in

Curiosities

a reference book. Ironbridge, in Shropshire, also explains itself. Bridges were not made of iron before the industrial revolution. They were not made of iron before 1779, in fact, for the bridge at Ironbridge was the world's first. It was constructed by the third Abraham Darby of Coalbrookdale, a member of a family which developed the use of coal-coke for iron smelting and did much to help on the industrial revolution. The bridge still stands. Another obvious mark of the industrial revolution is seen in a name such as Newmills in Derbyshire and also in Monmouthshire. Ironbridge reminds one of Ironville in Derbyshire, another late name. The interest here is in its ending. -ville is a characteristically modern ending for English place-names. It arises because of an early Middle English sound change which affected the southern counties. An initial 'f'-sound was voiced to 'v', and such pronunciations as *varmer* for *farmer*, *vine* for *fine*, and *vor* for *for* resulted, another example of 'Mummerset', the vaguely western dialect which serves on the stage and on television to characterize rustics of anywhere more than fifty miles from London. The frequent ending *feld* (field) was altered to *veld*, and later *vell*. It then became identified in people's minds with the *ville* ending, which is characteristically French: Charleville, Deauville, Trouville, and Joinville, for example. *Ville* means 'town', in French. It was therefore used for the naming of new English towns. In America a great many examples are formed from the surnames of their founders: Hopkinsville, Evansville, Madisonville, Clarksville, and so forth. In England examples are fewer because there was less opportunity to set up new towns, but there is Bournville, the village established for Cadbury's chocolate workers. Coalville in Leicestershire is another example. It is close to Woodville in Derbyshire; a place which was formerly Wooden Box Station, but changed to its present name in 1845. The Derbyshire volume of the Place-Name Society's survey notices that the original name was an allusion to the turnpike-keeper's hut.

Waterlooville in Hampshire looks like a new name on two counts: the 'ville' ending, and the presence of the name of a foreign battle as its main component. It might be thought that this was a direct commemoration of Wellington's victory, but Reaney says otherwise. It is named after an inn called *The Heroes of Waterloo*, on the London to Portsmouth road. (This sort of thing happens elsewhere; the Elephant and Castle district

Curiosities

of London came by its name in this way.) There are many Waterloos which are directly named from the battle, of course; there is a district of Huddersfield; a place in Dorset; and another in Norfolk. Other battles are commemorated also. The most obvious example of this is Blenheim, the magnificent palace which was built by the Duke of Marlborough out of money given as a reward for his generalship. The battle of Blenheim in 1704 was his most notable victory.

Some names have resulted from the revision of the boundaries of local government areas. There was an Act of Parliament in 1964, reforming the government of London, amalgamating many of the older London boroughs into a smaller number of new ones. It was interesting to find that the Minister of Housing and Local Government of the day specifically required the new names to be short and simple: 'complex names and artificial hybrids' were to be avoided. In most cases, traditional names were retained. The name of the borough of Newham, which was made out of East Ham, West Ham, Barking and Woolwich, was an exception. This was the final choice out of ninety suggestions. (The Town Clerk hoped that people would take care to pronounce the middle 'h'. It is unlikely they will.) The name of Haringey (including Hornsey, Tottenham and Wood Green) looks new, but is the most traditional name of all: it is a spelling of Harringay (part of the new borough) which is seven centuries old.

In the West Midlands, when five new county boroughs were formed, and were inaugurated in 1965, a similar solution was found for a new unit which incorporated Smethwick, Oldbury and Rowley Regis. It was given the name Warley: Smethwick had in it Warley Abbey, and the same name was found in the other two towns also. (The other four county boroughs preserved their old names.) Such names resulting from simple administrative convenience are not new. Camberwell, a district of London, has the authentic look of a genuinely traditional name, but it is no older than 1862. It was formerly known as Cambridge Town, after the Duke of Cambridge, but was altered at the request of the Post Office.

Though there are occasional oddities in English names, by and large where new names are created they tend to have the traditional flavour. Place-names have a linguistic style about them in this country which has acquired an air of dignity, even when the names themselves have meanings which were mundane enough

Curiosities

in the beginning. Mixon, in Staffordshire, has an air of Englishness which is not at all diminished by the knowledge that it refers to a dunghill. In America, where place-names are all much newer, there are such names as Commerce, Export, Enterprise, Oblong, Humansville; Wink; Sleepy Eye; Greedy Ridge; Baseball; and Frostproof. In England the traditional forms are sufficiently strong examples to mould most new names into the old pattern. There is only one obvious case where this has not happened: the village of New Invention, in Shropshire.

Chapter 9
Place-names and the English Language

The value of place-names to the historian should by now be clear. Their evidence is also important to scholars in another field—that of the English language, its history, and its dialects. From outside this may seem much less interesting than the concerns of history, where place-names illuminate battles and settlements, the occupations and beliefs of men and women, the sites of castles and of Roman roads. Philology is concerned with such matters as the date when a particular word first occurs, or the pronunciation of a particular sound at a given place and time. This seems altogether less lively. From the inside, however, things look different. Language is the one central skill which makes social living possible. Its alterations and varieties reflect different currents of human interaction. Investigating it, one is occupied with a study of very great interest indeed.

In the preface to his dictionary, Ekwall summarizes the linguistic importance of place-names under four heads. First, they often contain personal names which are unrecorded anywhere else, and so contribute to our understanding of Anglo-Saxon name-giving. Second, they often testify to the existence of words which are unrecorded elsewhere—words, that is, as distinct from names. Third, they show early examples of words which, though known to belong to the language in later times, enter the other records a considerable time after the date of the place-name. Finally, they help with the history of English sounds, especially in the various dialect forms which are so striking a feature of the English language. This last is very much more complicated a subject than the other three.

Personal names

Earlier chapters have shown how common is the pattern of place-names which is represented by such names as Barlaston (Beorn-

Place-names and the English Language

wulf's tun); Huddersfield (Huder's field), or Pelshall (Peol's nook) —that is, the pattern of 'somebody's something'. The first part of such a name is a personal name in the possessive case, and the second part is a property of some sort which he owns or occupies. How frequently it is met with may be illustrated by the larger settlements of Staffordshire which begin with the letter 'A'—a fairly random group for this purpose. Out of thirty-nine places looked at, seventeen contain personal names in this way. About half the names that occur on two random pages of Ekwall's dictionary do so too.

The Anglo-Saxon or Danish personal names which figure in place-names of this sort are of two types. The first is made up of two elements. Beorn-wulf, who had a tun at Barlaston; Broc-heard, who had a cottage at Brascote in Leicestershire; Thor-grim, who had a farm at Thorganby in Lincolnshire—these are a few. They are names like those of such Anglo-Saxon kings as Alfred, Aethelweard, Edgar, Edward, and the rest; or Anglo-Saxon writers such as Aelric, Wulfstan, Caedmon, and Cynewulf. Amongst the Staffordshire 'A's are to be found

Eadbald (Edboldestone, Domesday: Adbaston)
Ealdred (Aldredeslega, 1130: Adderley)
Eadmund (Aedmundeston, 1176: Admaston)
Eadgar (Edgareslege, Domesday: Agardsley)
Ealdred (Aldredeslega, 1129: Alderley)
Aelfred (Aluredstone, Domesday: Alstone)

The meanings of these personal names probably mattered very little. Each separate element once had a meaning, but in Anglo-Saxon times their combination in a personal name made nonsense as often as sense. *Frithwulf* means 'peace-wolf'; *Wulfgifu* means 'gift of the wolf'; Alfred means 'elf-counsel'; and Eadgar means 'prosperity spear'. That these literal meanings had no importance may be seen by the Old English pun on the name of King Aethelred. 'Aethelred Unraed'—'Noble counsel—foolish counsel' —is a joke precisely because it brings alive the latent meaning in the name. Had that meaning been wholly alive, the pun would have had no force.

The second type of personal name is shorter, composed of only one element. This was sometimes a shortening of the name of the double type above, but often not. From the Staffordshire 'A's again, we have:

Place-names and the English Language

APETON   Abeton. Domesday: Abba
ALTON   Elveton. Domesday: Aelfa
AMBLECOTE   Elmelecote. Domesday: Aemela

From other places we have:

FRODESLEY (Salop)   Frodeslege. Domesday: Froda's clearing
ISELL (Cumberland)—Ysala 1195: Isa's nook (Halh)
KEADBY (Lincolnshire)   Ketebi 1185: Keti's farm

Of these, Isa is not found in other English records, but there is an Old German name of exactly that form, and scholars agree that this is probably a similar name in English. Glevering in Suffolk may come from a name 'Gleawfrith', which is also unrecorded elsewhere but which is strictly parallel to another Old German name. Since Godric is a well-attested name, together with many others beginning in 'God'; and since Ealdhelm and many other names ending in 'helm' are also found in profusion, it seems highly likely that the combination Godhelm existed as an old English name. Nevertheless, it escaped being recorded. Godalming in Surrey (Godelmingum, c. 880) is a clear example of it. Other names which place-names alone preserve are Basa, to whom we owe Basingstoke; and Paecca, of Patchenden, Herts.

It is interesting to find that the names of women occur fairly frequently in place-names; the Staffordshire village of Apeton may have belonged to a woman called Aebbe rather than a man called Abba. On the borders of Staffordshire and Cheshire there is a small cluster of names of more certainly feminine nature: Audley, Balterley, Betley, and Barthomley, indicate forest clearings possessed by Aldgyth, Baldthryth, Bette, and Beorhtwynn.

Unrecorded words

Here we take together those words which are unrecorded completely, and those which, though attested at a later period, are first identifiable in place-names.

ALMONDBURY, Yorks.   Almanebire, Domesday. This is the burh of 'all men', or 'the entire community'. The first part is Old Norse, and is a genitive plural of a word which was probably *almenn*, meaning 'the community at large'. It was made up of *all* and *men*, but seems to be a single compound word

OLLERENSHAW, Derby.   This is the copse (shaw) growing with

alders. The first part is an unrecorded adjective made up of the well-authenticated word 'alor' (aldor) plus the adjectival ending 'en': *alren*

COCKHAMPSTEAD, Herts. COCK HILL, Wilts. COCKLE PITS, Yorks. These names contain a word *cocc* meaning a heap; which is otherwise unrecorded until the fourteenth century, when it occurs in the meaning of 'a heap of hay'; our modern word haycock

FORSTALL, Sussex. There is a Sussex dialect word *fostal*, meaning a paddock near a farmhouse, or a way leading to it; and together with the place-name this suggests an otherwise unknown word *fore-steall*, 'the place in front of a farmhouse'. The two parts of this compound word are well enough known

FOSSE WAY, FOSS DYKE, FOSS (river). These and similar names suggest an Old English word *foss*, a ditch or stream; but there is no independent evidence for it before the fourteenth century. There was a Latin word *fossa*, which gave rise to a British word, which gave rise to the Welsh word *ffos*: and at some point the Old English word must have been borrowed. The failure of this Old English word to be recorded seems merely bad luck

These are names which include otherwise unrecorded words. The following list turns the order round, giving the word first.

Pound The enclosure into which stray beasts were put. This occurs first outside place-names and compounds in the fourteenth century; in the twelfth century there had been the word *pund-breche*—the breaking open of a pound; and in Old English the word *pund-fald*, a pinfold. In place-names it occurs in Poundstock (Cornwall).

Shingle The small round stones which cover some beaches. This is not recorded before 1578, but there are various place-names which seem to contain it:
Chingford (Cingeford), Domesday;
Singleborough (Sincleberia), Domesday;
Shinglewell (Chingledewell), 1240

Spirt This modern English word for a jet of liquid is not found before the sixteenth century independently, but may well occur in such place-names as Spurtham in Devon, or Spirthill, Wilts. It would be a stream-name

Dimple This meant a hollow in the ground in the thirteenth century, a hundred years before it meant a hollow in the cheeks.

Place-names and the English Language

Before that, it is found only in place-names: Dumplington, Dimple and Dimples, all in Lancashire

Backstone This word is still used in many dialects for a flat plate used for baking oatcakes over the fire, but in former times it was obviously a flat stone. The first part of the word is a shortening of the word *bake*. There is no evidence for it before the sixteenth century, as an independent word, but place-names contain it from the twelfth. Backstone Beck in Yorkshire was presumably a good place to find suitable stones; Baxton Gill in Cumberland perhaps another. Baxenden in Lancashire and Blackstone Hall in Northamptonshire also contain the word. The last example is clearly a case of popular etymology

Catsbrain A name given to mottled soil, rough clay with stones, etc. Now found only in dialects. It occurs as a field-name in various southern counties in the twelfth century, but not otherwise until the thirteenth

The *Oxford English Dictionary* took no account of this sort of place-names evidence when it was first published, but the most recent *Oxford Dictionary of English Etymology* does. As the 'English Place-Name Survey' approaches its end, there will be further light thrown on the history of the English vocabulary.

Sounds and Dialects

To understand the importance of place-names for the study of sound changes and dialects, it is necessary first to know something of the history of language.

At all stages of a language, it changes; if it stops changing, it dies. The changes in the sounds used in speaking it are most important from the point of view of place-names, though there are other sorts of change also: words come into the language from other languages; grammatical conventions change; meanings change.

One set of sound changes going on today will give a first example. Thirty or forty years ago, the vowel sounds in words like fire, tyre, hour, flower were made quite clearly with two movements of the tongue. In *fire*, it moved first from the *a* position (as in such a word as 'hat'), to the *i* position (as in such a word as 'hit'), and then down to the unstressed 'er' position (as in a word such as butt*er*). In *hour*, it moved from the same starting position to the same finishing

Place-names and the English Language

position, but this time passed through the 'u' position as in *hut*. When occasionally one heard young people chiefly from the southern parts of England, and chiefly of the wealthier classes, pronouncing these words with all the same vowel, and this a simple long vowel as in *far*, it was something that (in the north, at least) it seemed legitimate to scoff at. 'There was a far in a tar fectry,' we used to say. 'It went on for arze and arze and arze.' We felt comfortably superior to these affected people. Today, however, such 'smoothed' pronunciations are much more prevalent, in all parts of the country. Prediction is unsafe, but this one is less hazardous than most: in another generation this new sound will be the accepted standard, and divergences from it will be classified as backward-looking and dialectal.

The points to notice about this example are that the change has affected all vowel-sounds that fall into the same type; it has proceeded to affect the whole community, but has taken about a generation to do so. Many other sound changes in the history of English have had all these characteristics. We 'catch' sound-changes from each other through the contact of speaking together. Another way of looking at them is as ripples in a pond. One set spreads out across the water, overlapping with other sets which have different starting-points. Each set takes time to complete itself and die away, but there are always new ripples coming along. The speech community as a whole is swayed by one fashion after another. A sequence of successful fashions adds up to linguistic history.

Suppose that one ripple of sound change fades out in the middle of its course: the result will be to create a boundary line to divide those who have been affected by the new style from those who have not. (In the past, before one man could ever speak to more than his immediate neighbours at any one time, it would be fair to think of the speech community as laid out over a flat area, susceptible to waves of change which moved horizontally across it. Today we have to think of vertical influences as well, exercised by the various mass media.) The lines where particular waves of change came to a halt, as many did, form the dialect boundaries. They can still be traced on the ground of England, and place-names are important evidence for this.

Waves of change, as might be expected, would slow down or come to a halt at places which imposed obstacles to communication as some natural barriers show. There are lines which can be

Place-names and the English Language

drawn along the Humber, and along the Ribble, which indicate the limits of linguistic features. What is surprising however is to find that though some changes stop at a barrier, others travel over it, and that each separate change requires to be mapped separately. The drawing up of a dialect atlas is a very complicated undertaking.

The social conditions which followed the Norman Conquest helped the development of a very rich pattern of dialects. English ceased to be the language of government or of education. A man who travelled away from his own manor on any sort of official business would probably need to speak French. The checks which might have held the change back, or kept wider areas of the country in line with each other, had been removed. The result was that the sounds of English, which already in the Old English period showed some dialect variations, rapidly developed a much richer pattern of differences. The language changed in other ways too—the grammar was much simplified, and numbers of old inflexional endings were swept away. New words were taken into the language profusely, chiefly from French. When, some centuries later, English became again the official national language, it was very different from the English of Edward the Confessor.

Sound changes are most important for the study of place-names, and both for the study of dialect. It is often difficult to know just how far over the surface of the country a particular dialect pronunciation spreads and place-names can often provide a clue. Take for instance words which contained the Old English 'y' sound. This has vanished from modern English. It is the sound that is used in French at the end of words such as *du* and voul*u*. To make it one pronounces a close 'ee'-sound, whilst pushing the lips forward into a position usually reserved for the 'oo'-sound. It was formerly found in words such as 'hyll' (hill); 'hrycg' (ridge), and 'mylen' (mill). During the Middle English period it developed in Kent and surrounding areas into an 'e'-sound. In the West Country and the West Midlands we find it spelled with *u*, and in the north and the east midlands it is found as *i*. As in course of time the speech of the South-East Midlands became standard English, most words containing this sound remain today in their *i* forms. Place-names, which may have had in this earlier period 'u' and 'e' spellings and pronunciations, have also been in many cases altered to conform to the standard. Nevertheless, the

Middle English forms sometimes survive today; earlier records show them more frequently. Examples are:

From the 'e'-area (Chiefly Kent): Helsted; Wormshill (in 1232 Wodnesell, perhaps meaning 'Woden's Hill'); Milton (near Canterbury) (Tun by a mill; Meletone 1242).
From the 'u'-area: Penkhull, Staffordshire (British name Pencet together with the English *hill*); Rudge, Gloucestershire (the ridge); Hulton, Lancs. (Tun on a hill); Milton, Staffs—tun by the mill—was formerly Mulneton (1227).

Examples from the 'i'-area are plentiful, though the earliest examples have often 'u'-forms, dating from before the distinctive East Midlands and northern forms developed.

A further example concerns the different fates which befell words of the Stretford-Stratford type. The meaning of this name is clear; the ford on or near to the Roman road. The element 'Stret' comes from the Old English word 'straet', which means a paved road. As we said in Chapter 2, only the Romans made paved roads before 1066, or indeed for a long time after. The source of 'straet' is the Latin *stratum*, borrowed into English very early. Now the vowel in 'straet' developed different forms in two areas of the country. In the south and west—the part in which was centred the old kingdom of Wessex—it remained as it was; but in the other areas it was raised to a long 'e'-sound. This happened a long time before the Norman Conquest, but later than the arrival of the Anglo-Saxons in England. Combined with a suffix such as 'ford', the first element suffered a shortening of the vowel; and the result was that the 'straet' forms gave way to 'strat', and the 'stret' forms to 'stret'. This accounts for the variations Stratford and Stretford. There are Stratfords in Bedfordshire, Berkshire, Essex, Middlesex, Wiltshire, Warwickshire, etc. There are Stretfords in Herefordshire, and Lancashire. A similar pattern can be shown by the Stratton-Stretton names, meaning 'tun by the Roman road'. Strattons are found in Bedfordshire, Dorset, Oxfordshire, Suffolk and Gloucestershire. Strettons are found in Cheshire, Derbyshire, Rutland, Leicester, Shropshire, Staffordshire and Warwickshire. To plot these names on a map would not give an absolutely clear pattern, but it would show the general shape of the dialect areas. The names preserve traces of sound changes which happened over twelve hundred years ago.

A more recent dialect change (but one which happened nevertheless a considerable time ago) is the voicing of unvoiced consonants in the south of the country when they occurred at the beginnings of words. Unvoiced sounds include 'f' and 's'; and these, in some southern dialects, are voiced to 'v' and 'z'. 'Varmer' for 'farmer', is a standard part of the actor's repertoire when he wants to sound like a Devon or Zummerzet man; 'oi zeed 'un' is what the 'varmer' usually is to be heard saying. These changes occurred in the twelfth century, and affected the areas south of the Thames and also the West Midlands, although the area where their results are still seen are more restricted today. Practically every place-name beginning with 'V' was brought about in this way, the chief exceptions being cases in which French words or names have been introduced as at Virley in Essex, which was originally Salcott Virley : one of those names in which the original place-name has had a family name added to it : or Vale Royal, in Cheshire, which is self-explanatory. Vernham's Dean in Hampshire was Ferneham in 1219; it means 'the ham among the ferns'. Verwood in Dorset was 'the fair wood'; Fairwod in 1329. Every name beginning with 'Z' in England was formerly spelled with 'S'. The interesting name Zeal Monachorum does not refer to a particular religious enthusiasm of the monks, but preserves the southern form of a word 'sealh', meaning 'sallow', or willow. South Zeal in Devonshire contains a word for 'hall'— Old English *sele*.

One very striking difference between the northern and the other dialects in the Middle English period was the pronunciation of words which contained the Old English long vowel 'ā', pronounced 'ah'. Over most of the country this became the sound in such words as whole, holy, goat, bone, stone and moan. North of the Humber it remained what it was until much later, when it became the 'a'-sound heard in the Scots pronunciation hame, bane (for bone); stane, and so forth.

The boundary between these regions was traced many years ago by Ekwall, using the evidence of place-names. Stainland, Yorks (Stanland, Domesday); Stainburn, Cumberland; Stainall in Lancashire, and many others, are all in the north. Stonydelph in Warwickshire (stony quarry), Stonehouse in Devon, Stoneleigh in Warwickshire and many others are south of this boundary. These all contain 'stone' as their first element; other examples could have been taken which used words such as 'oak' and 'broad' in them.

Place-names and the English Language

These are a few examples only of sound changes for which place-names give important evidence.

Before leaving the subject of dialect, there is one last point. It has been feared for many years by amateurs who have taken an interest in dialect that the influence of broadcasting and more recently television might be destructive. Many of these fears are excessive. It is highly unlikely that any such influence would rub out all dialect differences, though it is clear that they are able to diminish them perceptibly. One field however in which broadcasting has had a considerable levelling impact has been the local pronunciations of place-names. Fifty years ago, many places preserved distinctive local fashions. Slaithwaite in Yorkshire was pronounced 'Slowit', though probably never as consistently as its local patriots assert. Daventry was pronounced 'Daintry', Sawbridgworth in Hertfordshire is said to have been 'Sapsed'; and Uttoxeter in Staffordshire has sometimes been 'Utcheter'. Today, the generally accepted pronunciations of such places as these is that suggested by the spelling rather than that preserved in local dialect. In this change, broadcasting policy has had a good deal of effect. In the early days of the BBC, when it still had an Advisory Committee on Spoken English, it published a booklet advising broadcasters on particular difficult place-names. The principles behind it seem to have been to respect tradition as far as possible, but to recognize that most listeners would be more familiar with the printed form of the name than with the spoken, and that it would be simply misleading if the place written Slaithwaite were to be pronounced 'Slowit', for the benefit of its local residents only. The public at large would fail to make the connection between the two. This raises a nice issue of property —to whom does a name belong: the people who inhabit the place, or the world at large who need to talk about it? There is no property in names. Some pronunciations are more useful than others. It would not be easy to claim that, in the middle of the twentieth century, 'Slowit', and 'Sapsworth' and 'Daintry' and all the other traditional forms, were the only proper pronunciations, and they are certainly the least useful for the majority of people who do not happen to live there.

Taking it Further

We have written this book in order to introduce the reader to the enjoyment of the study of place-names, and of their relation to the life of people in the past. It is a big subject and this has been a short book. There is a great deal more to be said about it than we have been able to say. We must not leave the subject finally, therefore, without suggesting further reading.

E. Ekwall, *The Oxford Dictionary of English Place-Names* (3rd edition, 1947)

This is the one indispensable reference book to the subject, and a work of great scholarship. It lists a large number of names, and quotes their early forms and dates: it lists the common elements of English place-names; and it has an extremely useful introduction. Other writers, making specialized studies of one county or area, may disagree with occasional etymologies Ekwall suggests, but this is unimportant. Ekwall was one of the creators of place-name studies in England, and his dictionary shows his authority on every page.

P. H. Reaney, *The Origin of English Place-Names*, Routledge & Kegan Paul

This is a systematic survey of the whole field of place-names studies, by a scholar who has contributed much to it himself, having edited two volumes in the county surveys of the English Place-Name Society (Essex; and Cambridgeshire and the Isle of Ely). He is an authority also in the related field of family names.

Kenneth Cameron, *English Place-Names*, Batsford, 1961

Professor Cameron was the writer of the Derbyshire volumes for the English Place-Name Society—three of them. This book covers the same basic ground as Dr Reaney's book, and adds a useful table of common elements in English Place-Names. Both these books are to be highly recommended.

The English Place-Name Society, County volumes, Cambridge University Press

The English Place-Name Society published its first volume—*Introduction to the Survey of English Place-Names* by A. Mawer and F. M. Stenton, in 1924. Since then the various county volumes have appeared until at present about half the country is covered. It is interesting that, whilst the very early counties surveyed required no more than one volume, the later counties require much more. Dr Cameron's *Derbyshire* required three. The subject-matter grows with continued investigation.

More recent volumes have included information about field-names, which is an important supplement to that about the names of larger places.

Most larger reference libraries contain a complete set of the EPNS volumes so far published. They represent in most cases the fullest study of the local names available, and probably ever likely to be.

A. H. Smith, *English Place-Name Elements*, 2 vols., Cambridge University Press 1956

One of the early volumes of the Place-Name Survey's publications was a small book by Sir Alan Mawer entitled *The Chief Elements used in English Place-Names*, intended as a working handbook for collectors and investigators. Thirty years afterwards Professor A. H. Smith produced this replacement for it: a large two-volume work with a vastly greater number of entries, based on the work of the survey in the intervening years (for many of which he was its director). No one seriously interested in place-names can afford not to know it, and to use it frequently.

F. M. Stenton, *Anglo-Saxon England*, Oxford University Press

Sir Frank Stenton was one of the founders of the Place-Name Society, with Sir Alan Mawer. This, the standard history of the Anglo-Saxon period, covers the centuries when most of the

Taking it Further

English place-names were being established; and Stenton uses the evidence of place-names as part of the materials for his work.

F. T. Wainwright, *Archaeology, Place-Names and History*, Routledge & Kegan Paul, 1962

Dr Wainwright's short, austere book is a profound discussion of the problems of interpreting place-names, and the relations of place-name study to the two other scholarly disciplines named in his title. It is addressed to specialists, but it may be interesting to the layman too in showing what delicate issues may be raised by place-names in fields of great humanistic importance.

Index of Place-names

Abney, 79
Adbaston, 93
Adderley, 93
Admaston, 93
Agarsley, 93
Ainderby, 62
Aire, 13
Aislaby, 62
Alby, 62
Alderley, 93
Alice Holt Forest, 83
Alkham, 48
Almondbury, 94
Alstone, 93
Alton, 94
Alvden, 51
Alveston, 51
Amblecote, 94
Angmering, 31
Apeton, 94
Appleton-le-Moors, 34
Ardwick, 39
Arrow, 14
Arrowfield, 47
Arun, 87
Arundel, 87
Ashby-de-la-Zouch, 74
Aslacton, 67
Aston, 37
Astrop, 63
Audley, 94
Avon, 13
Aylesbury, 5

Backstone Beck, 96
Bakewell, 65
Balterley, 94
Barking, 90
Barlaston, 1, 92, 93
Barmborough, 68
Barmby, 68
Barmpton, 68
Barmston, 68
Barnby, 62
Barnoldswick, 39
Barrock, 15
Barthomley, 94
Basingstoke, 94

Bathurst, 1
Battle, 78
Baxenden, 96
Baxton Gill, 96
Beaconsfield, 5
Beamish, 76
Beaufront, 76
Beaulieu, 76
Beaumanor, 76
Beaumaris, 76
Beauvale, 76
Belgrave, 48
Belstead, 48
Belton, 48
Belvoir, 76
Berwick, 39
Betley, 94
Bettws-y-coed, 15
Bewick, 38
Bircholt, 36
Birtwisle, 85
Bispham, 32
Blackstone Hall, 96
Blagill, 57
Blanchland, 77
Blencarn, 16
Blencathra, 16
Blenheim, 90
Boggart Hole Clough, 52
Bonehill, 84
Bootham, 61
Boothby, 61
Boulge, 78
Bournville, 89
Boxgrave, 36
Brailes, 48
Brailsford, 48
Brailsham, 48
Bramingham, 84
Bramshott, 84
Brascote, 93
Bray, 15, 16
Breck, 57
Breedon, 15
Bremhill, 84
Brewood, 15
Brockhurst, 36

Bromlow, 7
Bromsgrove, 36
Brotherton, 68
Brounton, 34
Broxholme, 34
Buglawton, 51
Bugley, 51
Bulwick, 38
Burstead, 67
Burton, 67
Burton Stather, 67
Burton Thorpe, 67
Bury, 67
Butterwick, 39

Cadbury, 65
Castle Acre, 76
Castle Carrock, 76
Castleford, 75
Castle Howard, 75
Castlemaugham, 76
Castle Rising, 76
Castleton, 76
Castlett, 76
Castweazel, 85
Cam, 14, 87
Camberwell, 90
Cambridge, 41
Cams, 22
Cannock, 1
Canterbury, 3
Carlisle, 18
Catterick, 18
Cerne, 14, 16
Chadkirk, 44
Chapel-en-le-Frith, 78
Char, 14, 16
Charn, 14, 16
Chatham, 30
Chelford, 41
Chelmorton, 34
Cheriton, 59
Chesham, 5
Chester, 13, 23, 24, 65
Chetwode, 84
Chillington, 2
Chingford, 95
Chippenham, 60

105

Index of Place-names

Chiswick, 59
Cirencester, 24, 81
Claydon Botolph, 42
Clayton-le-Moor, 42
Clavering, 31
Clyst William, 84
Coalbrookdale, 89
Coalville, 89
Cockhampstead, 95
Cock Hill, 95
Cockle Pits, 95
Colby, 62
Collyhurst, 36
Conock, 2
Consett, 2
Cornwall, 17
Cotes, 32
Countisbury, 20
Cowdray Park, 78
Cowick, 38
Crake, 14
Craven, 17
Crawshawbooth, 61
Cray, 14
Creech, 15
Creedy, 16
Crewe, 21
Crewood, 21
Crich, 15
Crook, 15, 16
Crowhurst, 36
Crutch, 15
Culcheth, 22
Cumdivock, 21
Cumrew, 16, 21
Cumwhitton, 16
Cundall, 16

Danby, 63
Darent, 14
Dart, 14
Darwen, 14
Daventry, 101
Dee, 13
Deerhurst, 36
Denaby, 63
Denby, 63
Derby, 65, 66
Derwent, 14
Devizes, 78
Devon, 17
Didsbury, 67
Dieulacres, 77
Dimple, 96
Dimples, 96
Dinedor, 20
Dorking, 31
Downham, 37
Dragley, 52
Drakedale, 52
Drakehill, 52

Drakelow, 52
Dresden, 88
Droitwich, 39
Dumplington, 96
Dunham Massey, 74
Dunwood, 36
Durham, 81

East Garston, 68
East Ham, 90
Easton, 37
Eastrea, 31
Eastry, 31
Eastwick, 31, 39
Eaton, 37
Eaton Thorn, 48
Eccles, 45
Ecclesfield, 45
Eccleshall, 45
Eccleston, 45
Eddisbury, 8, 65
Egremont, 78
Elloughton, 48
Elmet, 17
Elva Hill, 51
Elveden, 51
Ely, 31
Ercall, 21
Etruria, 88
Ewshott, 82
Exley, 45

Faversham, 30
Fencote, 42
Fenton, 42
Ferrensby, 63
Fifehead, 83
Fifield, 83
Filey, 52
Firsby, 63
Fisherwick, 38
Fishwick, 38
Flashby, 62
Flixton, 59
Flotmanby, 63
Flowton, 68
Formby, 62
Forstall, 95
Foss, 95
Foss Dyke, 95
Fosse Way, 95
Fountains, 77
Frankby, 63, 65
Freefolk, 50
Freston, 29
Fretherne, 50
Frisby, 29
Friston, 29
Frodesley, 94
Frome, 14

Froyle, 49
Fulshaw, 36

Garrigill, 57
Gawsworth, 22
Gillingham, 30
Gledholt, 36
Glevering, 94
Gloucester, 81
Godalming, 94
Goodall's Corner, 88
Goswick, 38
Gracedieu, 77
Granta, 87
Grantchester, 24, 87
Great Barr, 15
Greenacre, 50
Greenfield, 3
Greenhill, 50
Grimley, 50
Grimsbury, 50
Grimsby, 50, 62
Grosmont, 77

Haconby, 62
Haltemprice, 77
Haltwhistle, 85
Hamps, 14
Hanworth, 82
Hardington Mandeville, 75
Haringey, 90
Harringay, 90
Harrowden, 47
Harrow-on-the-Hill, 48
Hascombe, 52
Hastings, 31
Hautbois, 78
Haven Street, 48
Haydock, 22
Haywood, 36
Heathcote, 42
Heathens' Burial Corner, 48
Heaton, 42
Helhoughton, 67
Hellaby, 62
Helperby, 62
Helsted, 99
Hescombe, 52
Hessenford, 52
High Ercall, 37
Hightown, 3
High Wycombe, 5
Hitcham, 29
Hobmoor Lane, 52
Hockerwood, 36
Hodnet, 21
Hoff, 48
Holbeck, 9
Holme Lacy, 74, 78

Index of Place-names

Holyport, 84
Hornsea, 90
Hounslow, 7
Huddersfield, 93
Hulton, 99
Hunmanby, 63
Hurdlow, 53

Ince, 21
Indescombe, 52
Ingleby, 63
Ironbridge, 89
Ironville, 89
Isell, 94

Jarrow, 81
Jervaulx, 81
Jesmond, 81
Jevington, 81

Keadby, 94
Kearsney, 78
Kedleston, 68
Kenn, 14
Kent, 17
Keswick, 59
Ketsby, 68
Kettering, 68
Kettlebaston, 68
Kettleburgh, 68
Kidsgrove, 36
Kinder Scout, 33
Kirby, 65
Kirkstead, 59
Kirton, 59
Knighton, 81
Knott Mill, 69
Knotton, 69
Knuston, 69
Knutsford, 69

Landican, 21
Landskill, 85
Laskill, 85
Laver, 14
Laxton, 34
Leadon, 14
Leeds, 6
Leicester, 66
Lichfield, 9, 85
Lincoln, 18, 66
Lindsey, 17
Liscard, 22
Llanberis, 21
London, 3, 18, 19
Lower Slaughter, 85
Lowestoft, 64
Lowleighton, 37
Lymm, 14

Lympne, 18
Mablethorpe, 64
Maiden Castle, 20, 75
Malpas, 78
Maltby, 62
Malvern, 15
Manchester, 19, 24, 65
Market Harborough, 66
Mautby, 62
Mellor, 15
Meopham, 30
Methwold, 37
Middleton, 37
Middlewich, 39
Middlewood, 37
Milton, 99
Mixon, 91
Moccas, 20
Moelfre, 15
Monkton, 32
Morchard, 16
More, 42
Morestead, 42
Morpeth, 85
Mossbrough, 42
Moss Side, 42
Moston, 42
Mountsorrel, 78
Mucklow, 7
Musgrave, 36

Nantwich, 39
Nateby, 62
Nether Booth, 61
Netherton, 37
Newham, 90
New Invention, 91
New Mills, 89
Newton, 37
Normacot, 63
Normanby, 63
Normanton, 63
Northwich, 39
Northwold, 37
Norton, 33
Nottingham, 66, 80

Oakford Fitzpaine, 75
Oldberrow, 38
Oldbury, 90
Old Castle, 38
Old Hurst, 38
Oldmixon, 38
Old Sarum, 38
Ollerenshaw, 94
Osberton, 67
Oswaldtwistle, 85
Otherton, 37
Ottery St. Mary, 77
Ouse, 5, 13
Overton, 37

Oxenholme, 57
Oxford, 41

Padbury, 34
Parkwalls, 51
Patchenden, 94
Pelshall, 93
Pen, 5
Pencoyd, 15
Pendlebury, 22
Pendleton, 22
Pendomer, 15
Penge, 15
Penketh, 15, 22
Penkhull, 99
Penkridge, 9, 15, 22
Penn, 15
Pennines, 15
Penrith, 15, 21
Penruddock, 21
Pentrich, 15
Peover, 14
Peper Harrow, 48
Pock Field, 51
Portsmouth, 4
Poundstock, 95
Prees, 21, 22
Preese, 22
Preston, 32
Puckeridge, 51
Purbrook, 51

Raby, 65
Ramsgreave, 36
Reading, 31, 59
Reagill, 57
Reculver, 18
Ridgmont, 78
Rievaulx, 77
Rose Ash, 84
Rother, 87
Rotherbridge, 87
Rotherfield, 88
Rowley Regis, 90
Roxborough, 65
Rudge, 99
Rugby, 63
Runcorn, 65
Ryedale, 77

St Albans, 19
St Michael on Wyre, 77
St Nicholas at Wade, 77
St Pancras, 43
Salisbury, 20
Salop, 80
Saltwick, 38
Sarum, 4
Sawbridgworth, 101
Scalby, 62

107

Index of Place-names

Scales, 85
Scarborough, 67
Scarisbrick, 57
Scarthing Moor, 51
Scholar Green, 85
Scholes, 85
Scole, 85
Scratby, 62
Scratgate, 51
Scratters, 51
Scruton, 68
Scugdale, 51
Seascale, 85
Seathwaite, 64
Seaton Delaval, 78
Shacklow, 51
Shapwick, 38
Shearston, 52
Shepton Beauchamp, 75
Shepton Mallet, 75
Shincliffe, 52
Shinglewell, 95
Shocklach, 51
Shopwyke, 38
Shropshire, 80
Shucknall, 51
Shugborough, 51
Sigglesthorne, 1
Singleborough, 95
Skinburness, 52
Slaithwaite, 101
Slaughterford, 85
Slawston, 67
Slingsby, 62
Smethwick, 90
Soulby, 62
Southrop, 63
Southwold, 37
South Zeal, 100
Spirthill, 95
Spurtham, 95
Stafford, 65
Stainall, 100
Stainburn, 100
Stainland, 100
Stainley, 8
Stainsby, 63
Stamford, 66
Stoke, 32
Stokesey, 78
Stonehouse, 100
Stoneleigh, 100
Stonydelph, 100
Stowe, 32
Stratford, 99
Stratton, 99

Stretford, 80, 99
Stretton, 99
Strixton, 67
Summerhouse, 61
Summerseat, 61
Summersgill, 85
Sutterby, 63
Sutton, 37
Sutton St James, 76
Swainston, 68
Swinden, 41
Swindon, 41
Swinefleet, 41
Swingfield, 41
Swinstead, 41
Swinton, 41
Sydling St Andrew, 77

Tadcaster, 24
Taddington, 34
Tamworth, 65
Tarporley, 35
Terrington St Clement, 76
Terrington St John, 76
Thames, 5
Thanet, 17
Thirlspot, 52
Thorganby, 93
Thorpe Arch, 64
Thrislington, 67
Thrumpton, 67
Thrusford, 52
Thrushgill, 52
Thrussington, 67
Thundersfield, 49
Thundersley, 49
Thundridge, 49
Thurloxton, 68
Thursley, 49
Thurston, 68
Tilberthwaite, 64
Toft, 64
Toft Monks, 64
Tottenham, 90
Towcester, 81
Trafford, 80
Tretire, 20
Trent, 5, 13
Trentham, 30
Treville, 21
Troughburn, 51
Trusey, 52
Tuerley, 49
Tusmore, 52
Tysoe, 49

Ugglebarnby, 62
Ullenhall, 38
Uncleby, 62
Upper Booth, 61
Upper Hulme, 57
Upper Slaughter, 85
Urmston, 59
Uttoxeter, 101

Vale Royal, 100
Vernham's Dean, 100
Verwood, 100
Virley, 100

Walpole St Andrew, 76
Walpole St Peter, 76
Wansdyke, 49
Warbreck, 57
Warburton, 65
Warley, 90
Warren Burn, 14
Warwick, 65
Watchett, 22
Waterloo, 90
Waterlooville, 89
Wednesbury, 30, 49
Wednesfield, 30, 49
Weedon, 48
Weeford, 48
Wenlock, 21
Wenslow, 49, 53
Werneth, 22
West Ham, 90
Weston, 37
Westrip, 63
Westwick, 39
Westwood, 3
Whichford, 29
Whiston, 29
Whyly, 48
Wichnor, 29
Wight, 17
Willey, 48
Wood Green, 90
Woodnesborough, 49
Woolwich, 90
Worcester, 81
Wormhill, 53
Worminghall, 53
Wormshill, 99
Wormwood Scrubs, 53
Wyeville, 48

York, 4

Zeal Monachorum, 100

For Product Safety Concerns and Information please contact our EU representative GPSR@taylorandfrancis.com
Taylor & Francis Verlag GmbH, Kaufingerstraße 24, 80331 München, Germany